A GATHERING OF
SPOONS

A GATHERING OF
SPOONS

The Design Gallery of the
World's Most Stunning Wooden Art Spoons

Norman D. Stevens
Photographed by Tib Shaw

Linden Publishing
Fresno, California

Cover design: James Goold
Design and layout: Maura J. Zimmer

ISBN: 978-1-610351-30-0

Printed in China

135798642

Linden Publishing titles may be purchased in quantity at special discounts
for educational, business, or promotional use. To inquire about discount pricing,
please refer to the contact information below. For permission to use
any portion of this book for academic purposes, please contact
the Copyright Clearance Center at www.copyright.com.

Library of Congress Cataloging-in-Publication Data

Stevens, Norman D.

 A gathering of spoons : the design gallery of the world's most stunning wooden art spoons / Norman
D. Stevens.

    pages cm

 Includes bibliographical references.

 ISBN 978-1-61035-130-0 (pbk.)

 1. Wooden spoons--Catalogs. 2. Wood-carving--Catalogs. 3. Stevens, Norman D.--Art collections-
-Catalogs. 4. Wooden spoons--Private collections--United States--Catalogs. 5. Wooden spoons--
Connecticut--Catalogs. I. Title.

 NK9705.S74 2012

 736'.4--dc23

                    2012028901

Linden Publishing, Inc.
2006 S. Mary
Fresno, CA 93721
www.lindenpub.com

1-800-345-4447

FRONTISPIECE:
Trygve Anderson
Texas
2008
Basswood

FACING PAGE:
French postcard c. 1935

1410. Nos Vieux Professionnels Bretons
Le Fabricant de Cuillers de Bois – Vente à la Foire

Collection Villard, Quimper

Dedication

To all spoon makers, past or present and known or unknown,
throughout the world for providing us with basic utensils that
may feed our body but are also often beautiful small sculptures
that feed our mind and soul. You bring beauty to our lives.

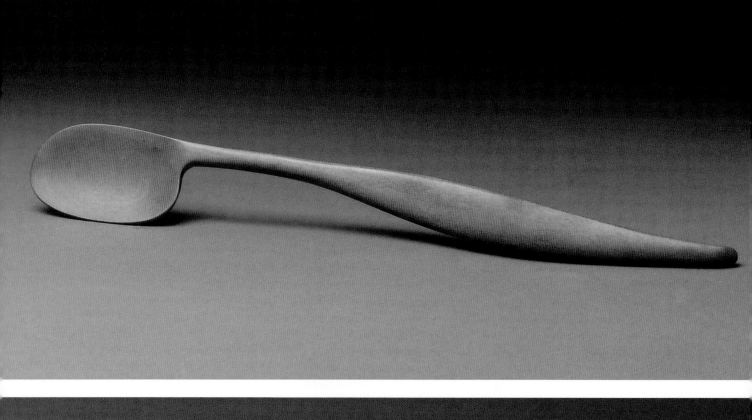

Contents

LEFT, TOP:
Richard Carlisle
New York
2009
Pink ivory

LEFT, BOTTOM:
David Hurwitz
Vermont
2007
Cherry

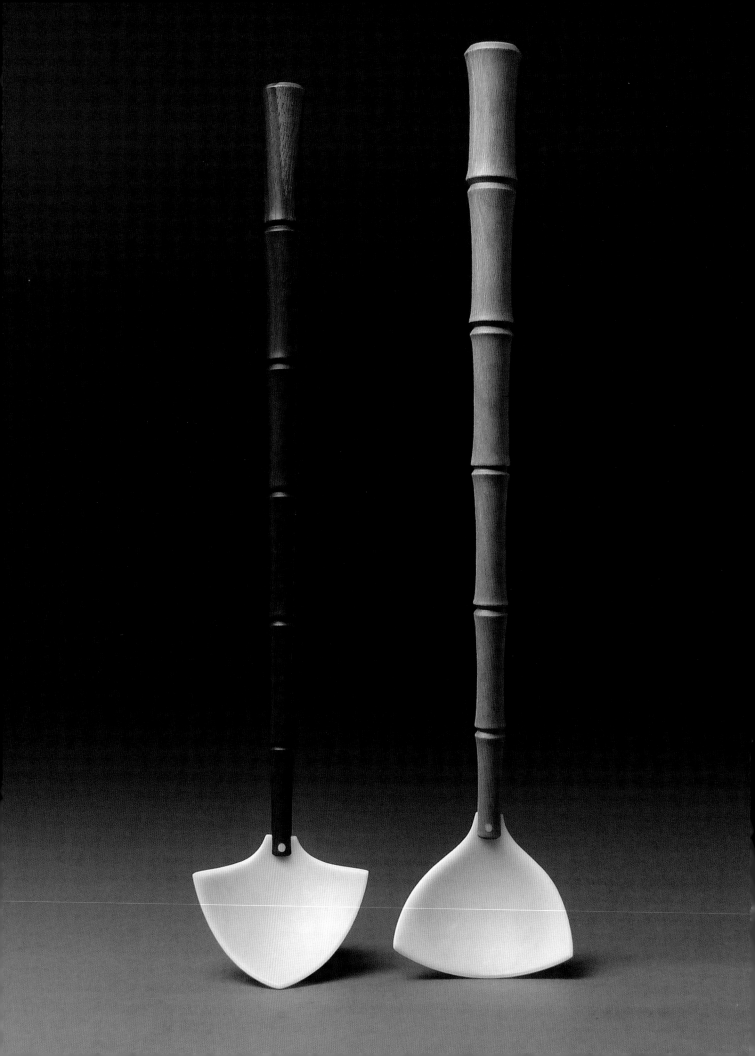

Foreword

A *Gathering of Spoons* has been an exciting endeavor for Norman Stevens and a valuable project for wooden spoon makers and future scholars studying the history of twentieth and twenty-first century craft. Norman explains the origins and development of the project but doesn't highlight his own considerable persistence, enthusiasm and dignity. He has clearly enjoyed the search, and the interaction with each participant that has led to many friendships. Though this is solely Norman's project, he and his wife Nora have assembled their significant collections with respect and kindness, making numerous friends throughout the craft world.

The wooden spoon is among the oldest of our essential functional objects. Contemporary amateur and professional spoon makers throughout the world continue to employ a variety of techniques, tools, skills, and wood species to produce examples of this form, often with inspired variations. *A Gathering of Spoons* provides a forum for, and elevates the stature of, this seemingly mundane utensil. It is a vehicle for skilled artists to create elegant functional and sculptural objects to be examined and admired. It defines the contemporary wooden spoon as an object worthy of serious attention by collectors and critics. Norman has had a valued partner in photographer Tib Shaw, who has undertaken the project successfully, understanding the challenge of portraying a long thin object in a single two-dimensional image.

This important collection, assembled between 2006–2011, demonstrates the remarkable variety of form and decoration possible when an everyday object is interpreted with imagination and skill. It provides documentation of early twenty-first century wooden spoonmaking, primarily in the United States, but with examples from more than a dozen other countries as well. Spoons in the collection range from those with functional folk character to highly sophisticated pieces intended as decorative objects. The use of many wood species presents a grand array of color, texture and figure. The impressive number of participating carvers reflects widespread interest by woodworkers in this traditional craft, and craft historians will undoubtedly profit from Norman's landmark survey.

A Gathering of Spoons also serves as a gathering of spoon makers as we become aware of others practicing our craft, thus providing mutual encouragement, particularly for those who work in isolation from other makers. We spoon carvers are grateful to Norman for his patronage, understanding of our work, and willingness to give it prominent recognition.

Barry Gordon and Norm Sartorius
October, 2011

Mark Gardner
North Carolina
2006
Ebony (left),
dogwood (right),
tagua (bowls)

The Education of a Collector

I was born and raised in southern New Hampshire. My mother, Ruth, hooked rugs and did intricate needle work. My father, David, had no mechanical skills despite the fact that both his father and grandfather were carpenters who operated a major building-moving firm. My parents were interested in antiques but the only collection they could afford to build was my father's collection of figural animal creamers, including a number by Royal Bayreuth and Schafer & Vater. In later years, my wife, Nora, and I found pleasure in adding to that collection often on trips to antique stores with my parents. I inherited my father's lack of mechanical skills and, after his death, his collection of creamers.

After receiving an M.L.S. (1957) and a Ph.D. (1961) in Library Service from Rutgers University, I began a career as an academic library administrator at Howard University and Rutgers before joining the staff of the University of Connecticut Libraries in 1968. Several years before I retired as Director of University Libraries at UConn in 1994, I began working a few hours a week as a reference librarian through a staff-sharing project. I continued to do so, and, for a number of years thereafter, also worked a few hours a week as a volunteer at the service desk in the newly established Thomas J. Dodd Research Center. That experience afforded me the opportunity to learn how to effectively use the emerging electronic search services and systems. Those skills have been critical in my spoon gathering efforts.

In addition to my academic library administrative career, I also made substantial contributions to the literature of librarianship dealing with library history, library humor, network growth and development, and library administration. I regularly wrote reviews of new publications in librarianship as well as, for many years, reviews of new reference books dealing with antiques and collectibles, crafts, decorative arts and a variety of obscure topics.

My career as a collector began in the early 1960s with picture postcards of library buildings. As that collection grew I added to it a wide variety of other library-related material, including commemoratives and souvenirs and other ephemera. My *Guide to Collecting Librariana* (1986) remains the only publication of its kind. In the early 1990s we donated the bulk of that representative collection, which then contained approximately twenty-five thousand library postcards and nearly five hundred

Anatolyi Kalinka
Lithuania
2008
Birch

commemorative or souvenir pieces, to the Centre Canadien d'Architecture in Montréal.

I also assisted Nora in building an extensive collection of women's handbags, purses, and compacts that she began in the early 1970s with the purchase of a box lot of purses at an auction. That collection now includes a number of one-of-a-kind purses by contemporary craft artists in the United States and England.

We have also been active members of the Connecticut Chapter of the American Book Collectors of Children's Literature and, until recently, I had been building what is probably the largest collection of children's books dealing with librarians and libraries as well as books and reading. That collection is now part of the Northeast Children's Literature Collection (NCLC) in the Dodd Research Center.

I was instrumental in helping UConn's University Libraries build a strong art collection that now, especially in the main library, provides a strong visual culture experience for users of the libraries. As part of that experience, I also helped develop and curated a considerable number of art, book, and craft exhibits in three major exhibit areas in the libraries on the Storrs campus. The last of those exhibits was *A Gathering of Spoons* in the Gallery-on-the-Plaza exhibit space of the Homer Babbidge Library in October through December of 2011 that included approximately two hundred and fifty items from the nine-inch teaspoon collection that will be described below.

All those collecting experiences helped me develop a considerable body of knowledge and skills that have proven to be invaluable in building my spoon collection, as well as other craft collections. A lack of formal education in any aspect of the visual arts has proven to be a substantial advantage as it has allowed me to pursue my own areas of interest, develop my own ideas on the craft field, and, above all, to learn from the many craftsmen whose work I have come to admire, respect, and, of course, collect.

Spoon Beginnings

After we moved to Connecticut and began exploring antique shows and stores, estate sales, flea markets, and other venues, looking primarily for library related material and purses, we realized that we could not afford to buy many of the antiques that caught our eye. I was vaguely aware of the League of New Hampshire Craftsmen's (LNHC) annual fair, and on one occasion in the mid-1960s we had stopped briefly at that fair while on a vacation. In either 1970 or 1971 we visited that fair again. Since then we have gone to that fair every year, attended special LNHC events like juried shows, and have been actively involved with the League. We now sponsor two awards (glass and metal) in the juried Living With Crafts exhibit at the Fair. More recently we helped the League take steps to expand its Permanent Collection that, since the League moved to new headquarters in downtown Concord, now has state-of-the-art storage space and an expanded display area.

Dan Dustin
New Hampshire
2006
Blueberry

The League was established in 1932, the same year I was born, and held its first fair in 1933. It grew out of an initiative by the Governor of New Hampshire that was designed to help lessen the impact of the depression on the state. It was built around a body of craftsmen in the state whose work was largely in the traditional functional mode. The League has kept strong ties to that tradition. Its members, more than those at any other craft fair that we have attended, have shied away from some of the modernistic extremes of contemporary crafts and from work that has moved far beyond any connection with or resemblance to functionality.

At about the same time that we began attending the fair, a number of new younger craftsmen had, for economic, political, and/or social reasons, moved to New Hampshire and become members of the League. Many of them were living close to the land, producing their own food, working in their sometime primitive living quarters, and often, especially those working in clay or wood, procuring their own materials. While our careers and life styles were quite different, we were roughly of the same age and shared a common educational background.

Three craftsmen in particular helped shape our tastes. Dan Dustin, a spoon maker, Dudley Giberson, a glassblower, and his then wife Betsy, a cloth artist, and Tia Pesso, a potter, were our guides. From them we learned to appreciate many aspects of the creation of their work and of the work itself. The visual appeal of Dudley's glasses or vases might attract us, but he always reminded us that the feel of a piece in our hand was equally important. Selecting the right glass to buy became a question of how a glass, the handle of a mug, or even a vase felt. Tia's work was entirely shaped by hand, and almost always bore the imprint of her hands, so it was often a greater pleasure to hold her work than to look at it. Thanks in large part to Dan, wooden spoons now have, for me, by far the greatest tactile appeal of any craft object. A major part of the attraction of a spoon is its feel. I regularly handle the spoons in my collection, look carefully at their details, and simply enjoy the way they fit my hand. As Jim Kustritz, a contributor to the collection, put it, "While others may aim mainly for visual appeal, my spoons are meant to please the hand as well as delight the eye. So few of the arts reach us through the sense of touch."

My fascination with wooden spoons, especially individually carved spoons, began when I met Dan Dustin, who was just starting his career as a spoon carver, on our first regular visit to the League of New Hampshire Craftsmen's Annual Fair in the early 1970s. His work first opened my eyes to the delight to be found in such simple utensils, and the pleasure to be found in establishing a lasting relationship with their maker. The ideals that I learned from Dan, and other craft teachers, have enabled me to develop the standards by which I judge contemporary crafts. I apply them, =in particular, in my selection and appreciation of spoons.

As best Dan and I can tell, we both began attending the LNHC fair in the same year. That first year Nora bought a small rectangular bowl from him and I think I bought a spoon; but I can no longer be sure if I bought my first spoon that year or the next. Nor can I remember which of his several spoons in my collection it might have been. The fact that Dan procures the wood that he uses to make his spoons, bowls, and occasional other objects, his reliance only on hand tools, his commitment to his craft, and his independence are what draws me to his work. Dan's ability to identify a spoon or a bowl in a piece of wood and then to release it is truly remarkable. I have never bought a piece, especially a spoon, from Dan without handling it several times and comparing the feel, not just of the shape but also of the finish, with other spoons in his booth.

Moving On

Over the next ten years or so, as I added a number of Dan's spoons to my collection, Nora and I acquired numerous other ceramic, glass, and wood objects. We also began to attend other craft shows, primarily in the northeast, on a regular basis. That included the American Craft Council's (ACC) Rhinebeck, NY show shortly after it began in 1972, and then all of the ACC shows in West Springfield, when Rhinebeck moved there in 1984, until that venue ended in 2000. We also began to attend other local and area craft shows, such as that in Guilford CT; and we watch for and visit craft galleries and shows wherever our travels may take us. I soon began to watch for other spoon makers and to purchase their work.

It was at a Rhinebeck show that I first met Norm Sartorius (http://normsartorius. com/) and purchased from him a straightforward tiger maple spoon with only a small amount of carving on the handle. That began a continuing relationship with Norm, and the purchase over time of a number of his increasingly complex sculptural spoons. He has become a good friend and a strong supporter of my spoon collecting efforts. He has, among other things, identified a considerable number of the contributors to the nine-inch teaspoon collection, and in many cases encouraged and persuaded them to make a spoon for my collection.

Without question, the most important precursor of the nine-inch spoon collection came from meeting Barry Gordon (http://barrygordon.com/) at the 1985 ACC West Springfield Craft Fair. I purchased a beautiful twenty-three inch cherry burl ladle, which has become even more beautiful as its color has darkened over time, from him.

Norm Sartorius
West Virginia
2006
Afzelia lay

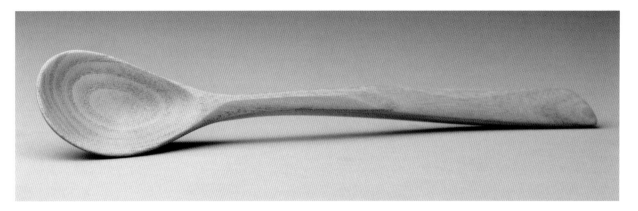

Barry Gordon
New York
2011
Elm

Barry described the creation of that ladle, and the forty-eight inch diameter burl from which it had come. In subsequent correspondence, I agreed to purchase, over time the twelve to fifteen spoons and ladles that he estimated he might create from that burl over the next year. Fortunately I can be patient for it was not until we visited Barry at his home in Baldwinsville, NY in June 2004 that the project was completed. In the intervening nineteen years seventeen different pieces had sporadically arrived in the mail, often unannounced. Now Barry had almost finished another seventeen pieces. We left the entire lot, which includes a mixture of utensils of all sizes, with Barry so that he could do some final finishing and have the collection photographed. A short while later the entire collection was shipped back to me. It remains one of the highlights of what has become an extensive spoon collection. Barry and I collaborated on an article called "The Spoon Project" in *Woodwork* (#92, April 1985, p. 60–63) that, accompanied by numerous color photographs by Rudy Hellman, describes the entire process in detail.

My final comments in that article are what finally led to the nine-inch teaspoon project. "I am also looking around for something else to keep me, and others, occupied over a period of time. One possibility is to find another good-sized but smaller burl—perhaps black walnut—that might be distributed to 10–12 spoon makers with the intent of acquiring a somewhat smaller collection of spoons all made from the same wood but each by a different craftsperson. At 72 I'm hoping that might not take another 20 years." Barry looked at a couple of burls and we discussed the possibilities several times. Ultimately we decided that, although the results might be interesting, the logistics of finding just the right piece of wood, cutting it into appropriate pieces, identifying contributors, distributing the pieces, and monitoring the process would be too complicated. So we abandoned that project but the underlying idea remained with me. I never realized that I would eventually turn it into the even larger and more complex nine-inch teaspoon project that will be described in more detail below. At 80, I doubt that I will oversee it for the next twenty years; but it has taken on a life of its own, and may outlive me.

An Interval

That idea of building a unique spoon collection lay dormant for a number of years. I continued to collect contemporary spoons on a small scale, and occasionally bought antique or vintage spoons through various secondary markets.

By the mid 1990s, I knew only ten or fewer contemporary spoon makers. I had met most of them and, as I have indicated, considered that personal contact, and the opportunity to handle their work to add a great deal to the acquisition of a spoon. I realized, however, that the effective use of electronic information services opened up a whole new range of possibilities. I had become a user of eBay shortly after it came into being in 1995, and soon discovered that contemporary carved wooden spoons, as well as antique and vintage spoons, were being posted there. That led to a number of purchases. As I further honed my information gathering skills, and as more and more new electronic services became available, I used those skills to identify a large body of previously unknown, to me, spoon makers throughout the world, especially as they built their own websites. The most valuable resource I found was Del Stubbs' Pinewood Forge website (http://pinewoodforge.com). About 1999/2000, he decided, after spending a winter in Sweden, much of it with the noted Swedish spoon carver Wille Sundquist, that he wanted to help other carvers around the world. Del did so by, as a toolmaker, making the type of tools used by Wille and other Swedish carvers. He also then began to provide a variety of electronic links to other spoon makers that remain the premier source of information about them. Through Del's website, I located Sue Robishaw and Steve Schmeck (http://manytracks.com/), homesteaders on the Upper Peninsula of Michigan, both of whom are wood artists and spoon makers. I soon had acquired a number of spoons made from a variety of woods by each of them. We have still never met but, more than any other of my initial electronic contacts, we have become close friends. The discovery that one-on-one electronic communication can establish a friendship has since enabled me to develop a number of similar friendships with spoon makers throughout the world.

In August 2011 Sue Robishaw sent me these comments on our relationship. "After many years of making, traveling, and selling our hand-carved wooden spoons at art fairs, we chose to take our creativity beyond the limits of that world. Steve settled in to carve one-of-a-kind bowls and spoons as he was inspired, and I explored box forms and spoons by the few instead of by the hundreds although watercolors soon drew me away. But how to market our work from our home in the north woods? We already had a website so we added our artwork; we were, at first, a bit dubious because we were used to personal contacts with our customers. One of our first contacts was Norman Stevens who purchased a small cherry bowl of Steve's in the fall of 2002, and next a spoon by each of us in July 2003. What a surprise and inspiration. Here was someone who truly appreciated what we could make from a piece of wood as well as the wood that it was made from. Not having met him in person [and we still have not met] turned out to be hardly noticeable. The freedom that his ongoing support gave us to work and sell from our home, and to create from the heart, flows through all of the carvings since then. Our relationship with Norman has also opened for us a wide world of fellow wood carvers that we had not known existed."

There is nothing like personal contact or, indeed, like the wonderful handwritten letters that I exchange with a few spoon makers, especially Ralph Hentall in England and Richard McHugh in Maine. With one or two exceptions, my electronic communications deal primarily with spoon related matters, and seldom deal with personal matters, or the interesting trivial asides, that personal contact and written—especially handwritten—letters provide.

Sue Robishaw
Michigan
2006
Wild pear

The Nine-Inch Teaspoon Collection

By 2005, I had identified a large number of interesting spoon makers. My thoughts then returned to the idea I had explored with Barry Gordon of assembling a special spoon collection. I spent a considerable amount of time pondering alternatives as I looked at, and handled, many of my spoons. My initial thought was to acquire from different artisans twelve to eighteen spoons that might be regarded as a table service for dinner with a group of people. Not, of course, that I had any thoughts of holding a dinner party of that size, or of allowing the spoons to be used as eating utensils. I also gave a great deal of thought to a set of criteria that would provide the semblance of the unity that a collection implies while allowing contributors the widest possible latitude. Ultimately I decided that length and bowl size should be the primary criteria. I owned a number of spoons that were approximately nine inches (just under 23 centimeters) long with a relatively small bowl, each of which fitted comfortably in my right hand. When held, the handle of those spoons nestled between my thumb and forefinger with the top of the handle resting gently on the fold between those two digits while the bowl was in a suitable eating position. A spoon of that length and size would, I decided, allow each contributor ample opportunity to exercise his or her skills in creating a small, sculptural object. The only difficulty I encountered, which was especially true with carvers outside North America, was in my use of the word teaspoon. In cooking terminology, a teaspoon is a defined measurement that is slightly smaller than what I envisioned. Ultimately, I described the size, when I was asked, as a spoon with a relatively long handle and a relatively narrow and shallow bowl. I also asked each contributor to sign, or mark, and date each spoon somewhere on the back and to identify the wood used for the spoon.

In October 2005 I sent the first invitation to eighteen spoon carvers. Their positive response quickly led me to abandon the idea of collecting a reasonable number of spoons. I soon began a more active process, which I still continue, of identifying and contacting as many possible participants as possible. By February 2006 I had received eight spoons and had contacted sixty-three potential contributors. As of October 2011, I have identified over five hundred spoon makers throughout the world, have received just over two hundred seventy five spoons, and have been promised about another seventy-five. In many cases I have incomplete or out-of-date contact information, in a small number of cases individuals are no longer carving or have died, but in only a very few cases have people declined to participate. I have not yet decided how long and how far I will carry this project. My goal, which I have largely achieved, has been to build a collection that is representative of the state of spoon making in the world in the first part of the twenty-first century.

The nine inch criterion is the only one to which I have strictly adhered. While most of the spoons have an eating utensil sized bowl, some have a larger bowl. A number of the spoons are primarily sculptural and clearly not designed as an eating utensil. All of them, however, have recognizable spoon elements. Not all of the contributors have signed and dated their work either as an oversight or as a matter of personal principle. I also ask contributors to send me whatever information is available about themselves, their spoon, the wood they used, and their techniques including the finishing process. That information has varied widely.

As the collection began to grow, I indicated that I was especially interested in spoons made from an unusual wood, or from wood with a story behind it. That request has resulted in the acquisition of spoons made from poison ivy (Sue Jennings), pistachio (John Scariano), a rose bush (Aaron Clapp), and other exotic trees, shrubs, or plants. It has also brought spoons with a special history. Donna Banfield created a simple spoon from a maple tree that grew outside the window of the farmhouse in New Hampshire where Robert Frost lived in the early 1900s when he wrote his poem "Tree at My Window." Ralph Hentall sent me a spoon made from an oak beam that dates back to the fourteenth century, from Lambeth Palace, the home of the Archbishop of Canterbury.

Each spoon is numbered and given a tag with the maker's name and state or country, the type of wood, and the date received. It is then placed in a numbered cloth bag both to protect it and to assist in locating a particular spoon. From the beginning of the project, I have maintained extensive documentation for each actual or potential contributor, largely in paper files, that include printouts of e-mails as well as written correspondence, photographs, biographies, catalogs, and other information. I maintain three computer files. The first is a list of the contact information for all of the spoon makers I have identified. Annotations indicate whether they have declined, promised, or participated in the project as well as notes about death or retirement. The second is a chronological/numerical list arranged by the assigned number. That list includes the maker's name, state or country, type of wood, and year received. I also maintain a numerical card file in which I maintain a record of cost and a tally of the cumulative and average cost. The latter remains at slightly less than $100. The third, and most significant, file is an alphabetical catalog which contains a short entry for each contributor that includes information about the person, his or her background, the spoon, and in almost every case some comments based on my personal reaction to the spoon. In each case I share a draft with the maker and revise it based on any comments, corrections, or suggestions that he or she may have. It has not been possible, because of the size of that file, to include it in this book and, in any case, it, like the collection, continues to grow.

I am often asked if I have a favorite spoon. My response is that each of the spoons has its own special appeal that may have to do with my relationship to the maker, the story behind the spoon, or simply its tactile and visual appeal.

The following is an example of the kind of entry that I prepare accompanied by a few images sent by the maker that have been added to his file. Documenting each spoon carefully, and maintaining as an extensive a file as I can, along with the range of information that may be found on the Internet, is an essential element of my collection.

Martin Damen

In February 2011, Sally Dodson, of the Heritage Craft Association in Great Britain, gave me contact information for a half dozen HCA members who make spoons, including Martin Damen. An immediate positive response led to a clarification of the size and a comment that "I like to follow traditional practice and use what [wood] is available locally…. At the moment I have some cherry plum (still nice and green)." In early September, as we had agreed upon, a box arrived with two spoons, a brief descriptive letter, and a disc with images of Martin, his tools, and the spoons. He describes himself as a traditional green woodworker, and his website (www.martin-damen. co.uk) indicates he has been practicing traditional woodwork since 2000. He initially made rustic furniture and field items, such as gates and hurdles, but now produces spoons, bowls, and platters using only simple hand tools. He also uses a traditional pole lathe to make a variety of domestic items and

Martin Damen

other products. He wrote, "Originally I had intended a more formal and symmetrical design inspired by European spoons of the 16th–17th centuries. However, in the event the cherry plum (*Prunus cerasifera*) was not suitable for the proposed design. Consequently your free form spoon evolved from a twisted piece of branch wood. I have left the spoon 'off the knife' (i.e., without sanding) as this is my normal practice and have finished it with food grade linseed (flaxseed) oil." The darker color running down the center of the handle on the front of Martin's unsigned spoon, with just a touch at the bottom of the bowl, immediately attracts the eye as does the shape of the top of the handle. The 'off the knife' finish is smooth but with, in places, just enough texture to give an appreciation of the technique. Finally, and most importantly, it fits my hand remarkably well. Held between my thumb and forefinger, my forefinger rests neatly on the bottom of the handle just above the bowl; the curvature of the bowl is such that it would be ideal lifting food to my mouth; and the curvature of the top of the handle clearly was also made to accommodate the hand. The cherry plum spoon was carved using only an axe, a straight knife and a hook knife.

The second smaller spoon was created using wood from a 222 year-old oak, felled in January 2010. The oak was located at Blenheim Palace, the ancestral home of Sir Winston Churchill. The tree, named OneOak, is now being used in an educational project (www.sylva.org.uk/oneoak).

Oak is not normally used for spoon making so Martin boiled it for two hours with several changes of water and then left to dry thoroughly. So, in effect, the spoon was "tanned," creating its dark color. Once dry, the spoon was sanded by hand finishing with 1500-grit paper and finished with food grade linseed oil. A much smaller spoon, it would fit a young person's hand remarkably well.

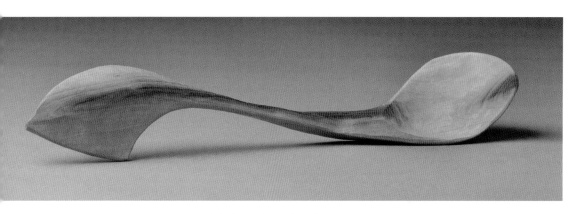

LEFT:
Martin Damen
England
2011
Cherry plum

RIGHT:
Martin Damen
England
2011
Oak

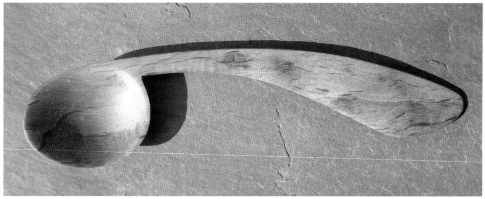

A Tribute to Spoons and Their Makers

In today's craft world the predominant notion seems to be that the bigger, more abstract, and expensive an item is the better it is. The goal sometimes seems to be for the artisan to create a "signature" piece that will be recognized instantaneously as his or her work. Why then should anyone collect spoons? Why did I decide to adopt these orphans?

The first primitive spoons date back to the Stone Age when stone tools were used to create a simple, hollowed-out vessel. Richard McHugh, a contemporary Maine spoon maker, describes making his first spoon when, as a young boy playing in the yard, he took a sharp stone and a stick to create a spoon that he then "sanded" by rubbing it against a granite step. While over time metal spoons replaced wooden spoons, especially in industrialized countries, for thousands of years wooden spoons have been a basic cooking and eating utensil. As recently as 1912 in the province of Nizhnii Novgorod in Russia, for example, over eighteen thousand people produced two hundred million spoons.

While wooden spoons continue to be designed and created as practical utensils, our human desire to decorate, or adorn, almost anything can be seen in the wide range of decorative spoons that often reflect cultural, societal, or tribal customs, designs, and symbols. There have long been spoon carvers who make substantial quantities of spoons for sale, but in a great many instances, individuals have carved, and continue to carve, wooden spoons simply for family use. An 1881–1883 diary, kept by Gotham Bradbury in the Cincinnati area, describes his household tasks as including making wooden spoons for cooking.

In an earlier effort to describe and categorize wooden spoons, I came up with a dozen or so categories (e.g., tribal spoons) but was soon persuaded that there was so much overlap that it would be impossible to develop anything approaching mutually exclusive categories. In many parts of the world, wooden spoons are still the basic eating utensil and, in addition to those created by a family for its own use, there are "professional" artisans who produce and sell spoons, to serve the needs of their community. Those spoons often contain cultural elements or reflect a particular tradition. In our so-called "civilized" countries metal spoons, and tableware, have long been the norm, although there has always been a role and demand for wooden spoons, especially as cooking utensils. An increasing quantity of low-cost, mass-produced wooden spoons are now readily available in super markets, cooking and food stores, and other locations. There are a few higher quality, and slightly more expensive, semi-mass produced wooden spoons available in gift shops, galleries, and high-end cooking stores. There are still, fortunately, any number of individual spoon makers, many doing high quality work, who are creating spoons for their own pleasure and use, and/or to share with family and friends. Finally, there are a considerable number of craftsmen who seek to make their living, in whole or by part, by creating distinctive wooden spoons of their own design and style and selling them in a variety of venues ranging from a local farmers market, to craft galleries and fairs, their own websites, or electronic stores such as eBay and Etsy. Their work, with a few notable exceptions, such as Norm Sartorius and Jacques Vesery, appears to exist largely outside the ken of the fine art establishment.

My collection consists of spoons from many different cultures and traditions created by talented artisans at all levels. A generally low profile has enabled them to develop their own approach to their work, and to create distinctive and often imaginative work. I salute them. I feel fortunate to have found them, collected their work, supported them, and—as a number of them have suggested—brought their attention to the work of others thus inspiring them to expand their horizons.

The virtues of wooden spoons are many. A spoon typically reflects the closest relationship that exists between the material and the artist in any medium. The wood that a carver uses frequently comes from his or her own property, and is often made from salvaged wood or a dead tree. It is not uncommon for it to be made from a piece of firewood that has been rescued as it was being put on the fire. In his article "Finding the Wood" (*Woodwork* June 2003, p. 51), Michael Cullen extols the virtues of finding wood using, as one example, the harvesting of some mountain mahogany, from which my spoon was ultimately made, at 3,000 feet on Mount Shasta in Oregon. A painter may depict an identifiable scene but only a few craftsmen, including a number of spoon makers, can tell you precisely where the materials used in their work came from.

In numerous cases the wood may come from a tree that has a special significance for the carver, as in the case of Sharon Littley's Mother Goose spoon, the wood for which came from a plum tree that had grown in her father's yard for many years. A number of carvers use wood from invasive trees or vines like buckthorn or English ivy that have been cut down to help prevent their spread. Jude Binder's splendid swirl spoon was carved from a maple sapling that had been choked by a vine whose spiral tendrils contributed to the pattern that she uncovered in the wood. A substantial number of the spoons in the collection have a special story behind their creation. Russ Cherry carved his spoon from the wood of a privet bush that he had removed while clearing land on his farm. When he finished the spoon, the first spoon he had ever made from privet, he did not like its plain white color. Then he remembered that the yellow root plant that had been growing around the bush he removed had commonly been used to make a dye. He collected some of it from which he made a dye that he used to give his spoon its exceptional yellow finish, thus reuniting the two plants that had grown together for a number of years.

In a short piece that Edwards Smith sent to me he wrote, "Wooden spoons make excellent gifts. People especially love it when the wood is from a tree or a limb that they gave to you. Almost any limb wood can produce a good spoon blank. Using 'their' wood provides people with a connection to nature that they had known and come to love. The tree may be gone but the memory of it survives in a spoon that can be passed on from generation to generation."

Because only a small piece of wood is needed to make even the most elaborate spoon, spoon carvers can use the most diverse variety of basic materials of any craftsman. The contributors to the collection have done an excellent job of responding to my appeal to create their work from a wood not already represented in the collection. More than 110 different species are now represented. In using a wide diversity of woods, the contributors have also pushed their skills and their imagination to find the spoon in the wood, to set it free, and to create a sculptural object—no matter how simple or elaborate—that has both tactile and visual appeal. No two spoons are exactly alike even those that come from a common tradition, like Swedish spoons, whether from Sweden or Minnesota, thus providing the widest possible diversity. In the many cases where I have several other spoons from the same carver, it is often possible to identify all of them as having been made by the same person, but even in those cases each spoon has its own distinctive appearance and personality.

Barry Gordon reminded me that there is a considerable range of methods, both with and without the aid of electricity, used by spoon makers. These methods range from the simple spoon created from green wood using just a few hand tools to, in a few cases, lathes. A variety of finishing techniques are also employed ranging from no sanding (off the knife), to an assortment of scraping and sanding variations, and, finally, a substantial variation in finish coatings depending, in part, on whether or not the spoon is intended as an eating utensil. The end result is that from start to finish each spoon maker utilizes his or her own techniques, thereby adding yet another personal element to the enjoyment of a spoon. Different woods—even, for example, the wide variety in the figure of wood from different maple trees—different techniques, different finishes, different designs, different signatures or marks, and different traditions have produced an assortment of spoons that I could never have imagined.

I believe strongly that here is a craft tradition that deserves to be continued but is too often ignored. No matter how abstract, complex, non-functional, or unusual a spoon may be, it carries with it a long history and tradition. At the same time, a considerable number of spoons equal in design and execution the best work of any other contemporary craftsmen. This link with the past is an important element of high quality work that looks to the future.

In addition to establishing new friendships, I feel fortunate that I have, in some small way, been able to identify the depth and breadth of the work of spoon makers in many parts of the world in building this collection. I have also helped bring together a community of artisans, many of whom work in settings outside the bounds of the established craft world. I have also helped challenge them to look towards improving their skills and expanding their imagination.

To My Readers

Apart from the pleasure of finding a new spoon maker, and acquiring a new spoon, I am always delighted to meet, even electronically, that person. In the process of building my spoon collection, I have made many new friends who continue to keep me informed about their work and their activities. Many of the spoon makers whose work was featured in the American Association of Woodturners (AAW) catalog *A Gathering of Spoons*, which was published in connection with an exhibit in 2010 first at the AAW Gallery of Wood Art and subsequently at its Symposium in Hartford, CT, have told me that seeing the work of so many other spoon makers has challenged them to improve their skills and expand their horizons. I hope that this book will provide additional encouragement to all spoon makers. I have also been pleased to be able to provide modest financial support to the spoon community, and to call attention to the work of spoon makers throughout the world.

I am pleased to be able to share my passion for spoons with other collectors and to the public through my periodic updates, exhibitions of spoons from the collection, and now the publication of this book. I will be delighted to hear from all readers of this book about anything having to do with the contemporary spoon world.

Finally, I would like to encourage all readers, especially members of the general public, to seek out and support the spoon community. The new interest in supporting local food producers, the growth of farmer's markets, special local dinners, and cooking activities and events, has brought with it an increase in the marketing and sale of wooden spoons and other utensils, in both major chains and local stores. In too many cases those factory-produced utensils, while they may be perfectly fine for stirring a pot, lack tactile and visual appeal. I would urge you to seek out and support local spoon makers as avidly as you seek out and support local food producers. Encourage the farmer's markets you attend, the local galleries and gift stores you patronize, and similar venues to make the spoons, and other utensils, of local craftsmen available.

Finally, of course, I hope that this book will encourage others to become serious spoon collectors. A good quality contemporary spoon collection, perhaps designed to reflect a particular interest (e.g., work from a particular state, region or country, or in a particular style or tradition such as lovespoons), can be built at a reasonable cost, requires minimal space, is easily transportable, and can be enjoyed by the hand and eye.

Photographing Spoons

Every good spoon, whether intended solely for practical use or conceived of as art, is a small sculpture. Meant to be enjoyed from all angles, it is additionally held in the hand, hefted and tilted. Thus photographing spoons, particularly when only one view will be published, is a challenging exercise. As a photographer, my goal was to present the single most informative view of each spoon—to highlight its best qualities, and to show the form completely as possible.

My technique centers on simplicity; I most often use only one light source and reflectors, because that is what nature provides, and I feel that it complements natural materials. I also keep the background and angles simple to ensure that the object is what is noticed, not the photography. That said, I light and position each piece carefully, because although "the camera never lies," it does perceive things differently than we do, a factor that needs to be overcome in creating an image accurate to our eyes.

I feel honored to have been trusted with exhibiting and photographing the spoons in this collection. I have been privileged to have the opportunity to handle each and every one of them. The images in this book serve to document the amazing range in contemporary spoon carving. My fondest hope is that they may also create an awareness and appreciation that leaves readers hungry to touch (and perhaps carve) the real thing.

—*Tib Shaw*

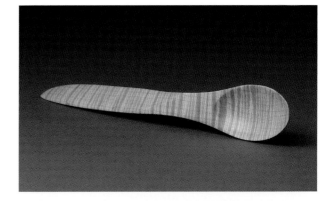

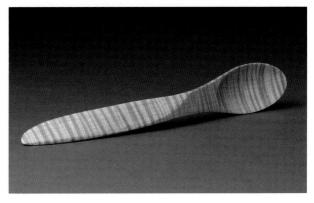

"A shift in angle and lighting reveals the planes of the handle." Mark Stanton, PA, 2010, tiger maple. Top image is the before, bottom the final image.

A GATHERING OF
SPOONS
DESIGN GALLERY

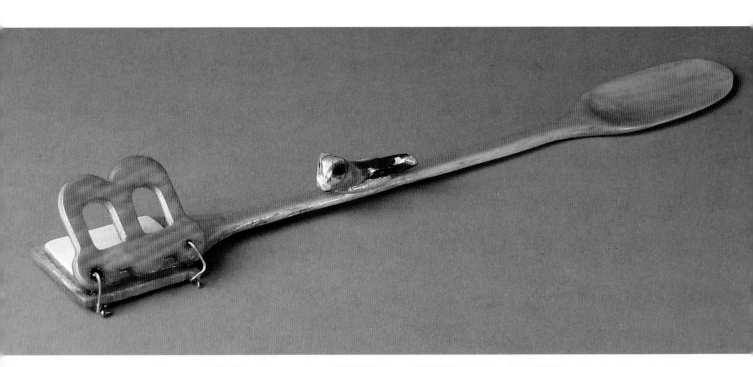

TOP:
Tony Abbott
Kentucky
2008
Pine

ABOVE:
Joseph Albert
Washington
2006
Alder

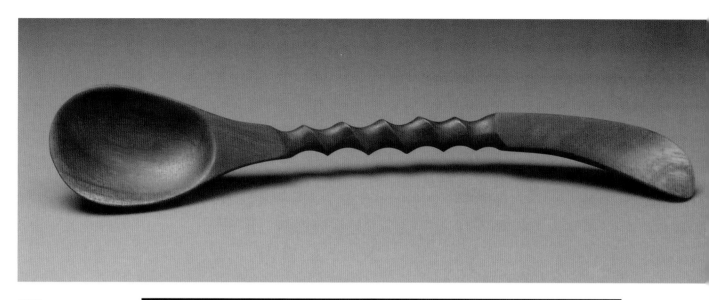

ABOVE:

Jim Anderson
Minnesota
2009
Koa

LEFT:

Trygve Anderson
Texas
2008
Basswood

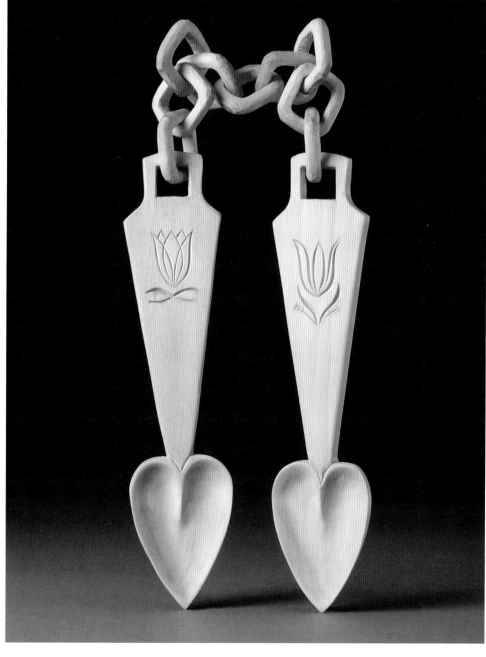

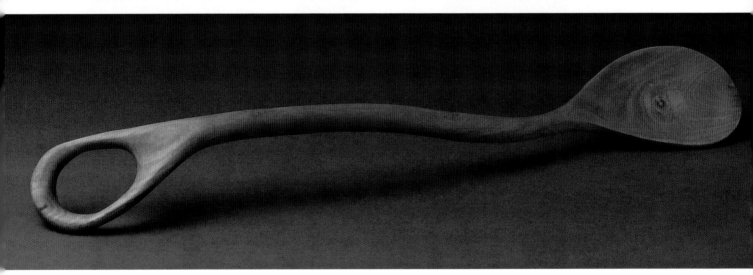

TOP:
Steven Antonucci
New Jersey
2010
Desert ironwood

MIDDLE:
Sergey Appolonov
Russia
2010
Sea buckthorn

ABOVE:
Todd Aubertin
New Hampshire
2010
White mulberry

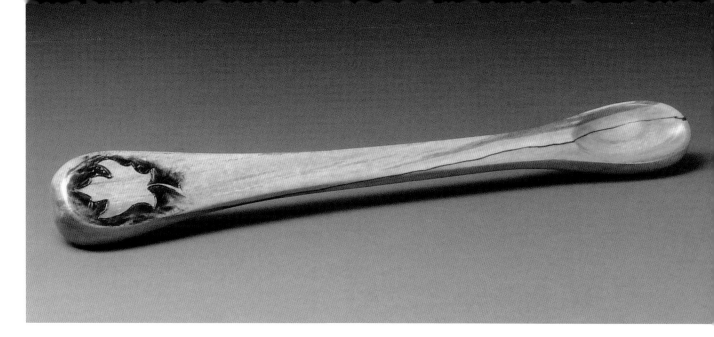

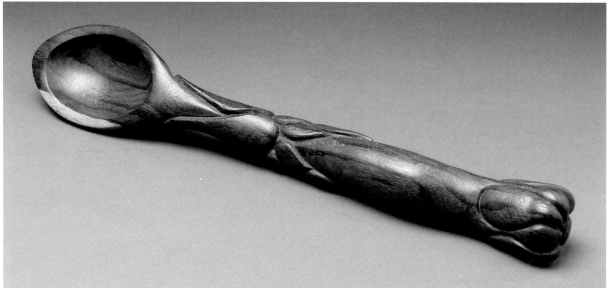

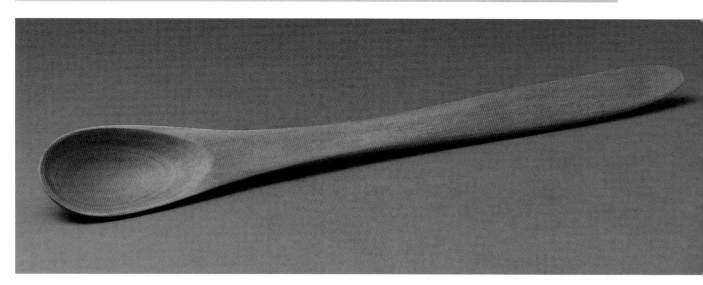

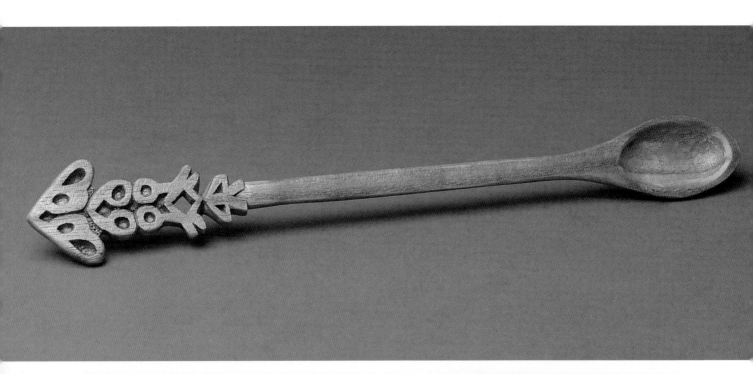

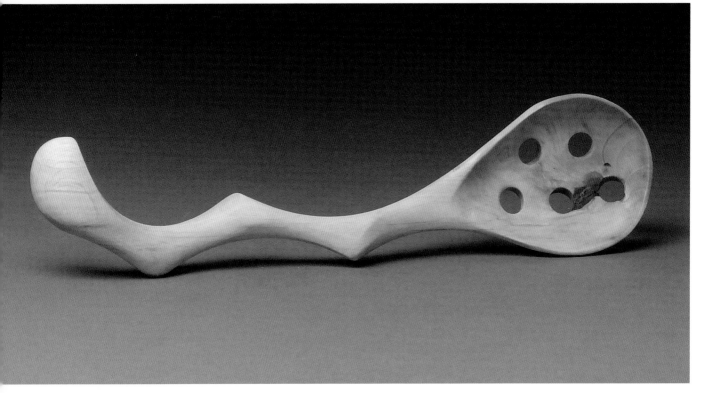

TOP:

Bev Beatty
West Virginia
2007
Catalpa

ABOVE:

Espri Bender-Beauregard
Indiana
2011
American hornbeam

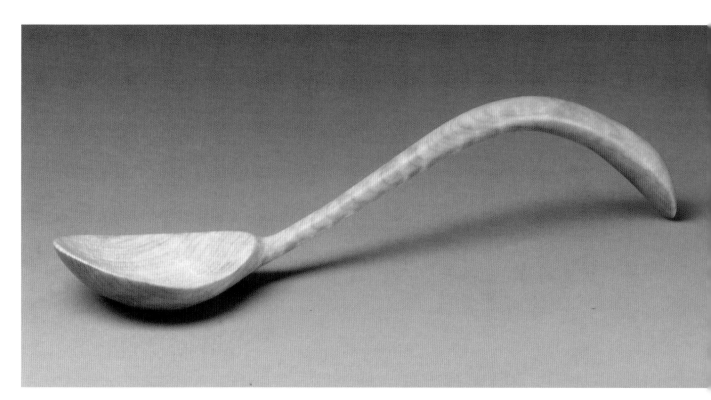

TOP:
Shawn Bills
Vermont
2011
Maple

ABOVE:
Jude Binder
West Virginia
2008
Maple

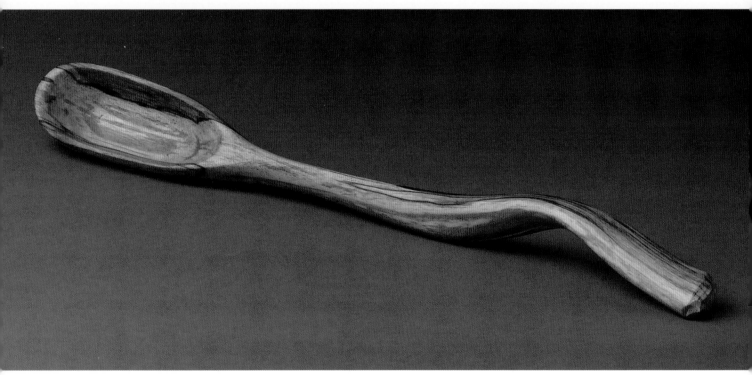

TOP:
Elia Bizzarri
North Carolina
2006
Dogwood

ABOVE:
Sage Blanksenship
West Virginia
2008
Spalted alder

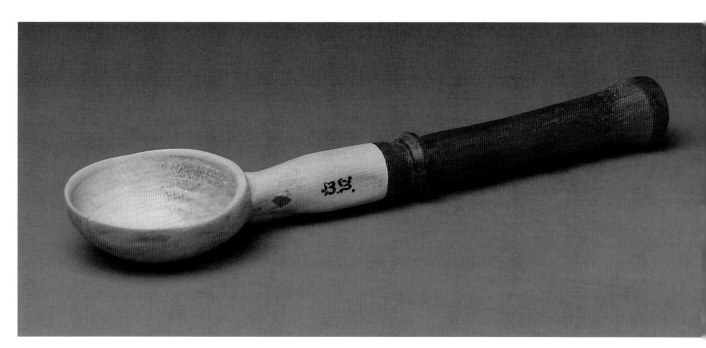

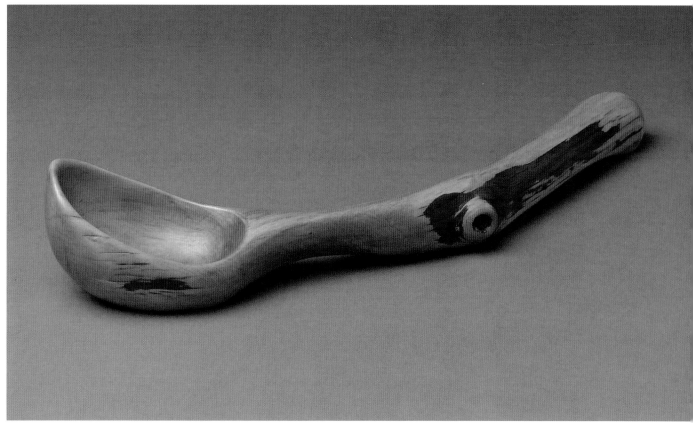

TOP:
Jeffrey Blind Horse
California
2007
Ash, bloodwood

ABOVE:
Meg Boden
Connecticut
2009
Laurel

TOP:

Campbell Bosworth
Texas
2006
Mesquite

ABOVE:

Paul Burke
Massachusetts
2006
Teak

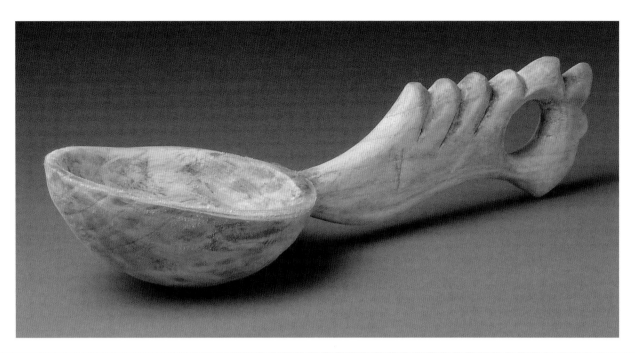

TOP:

Alexandru Buturus
Romania
2008
Linden

ABOVE:

Mike Byram
Indiana
2009
Chestnut

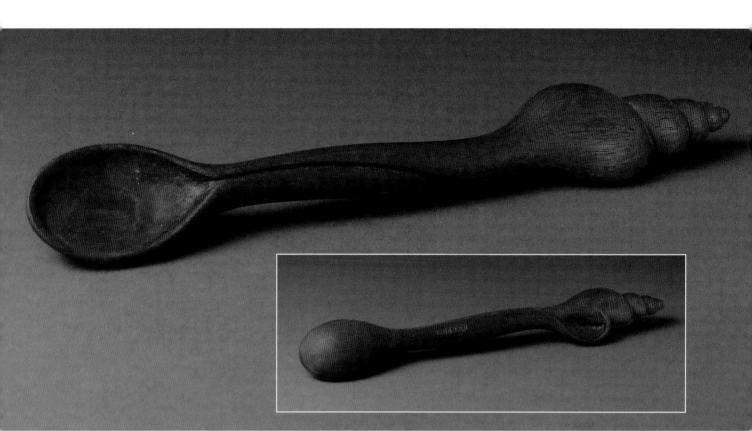

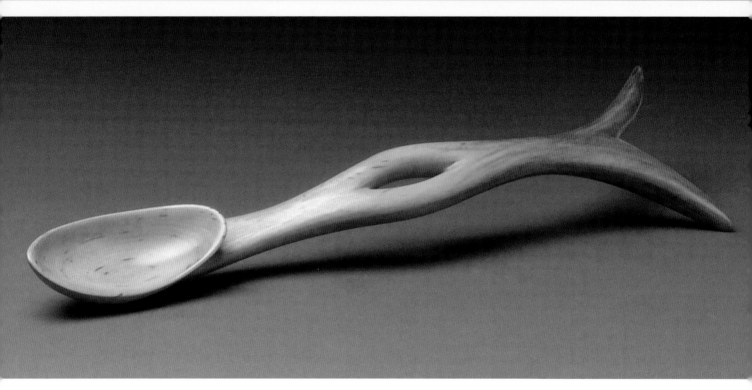

TOP:

Susan Caban
Puerto Rico
2008
Mahogany

ABOVE:

Patrick Cahill
Minnesota
2010
Ironwood

Richard Carlisle
New York
2007–2011
Hawthorn, pink ivory,
snakewood

ABOVE:

William Chappelow
California
2006
Mesquite

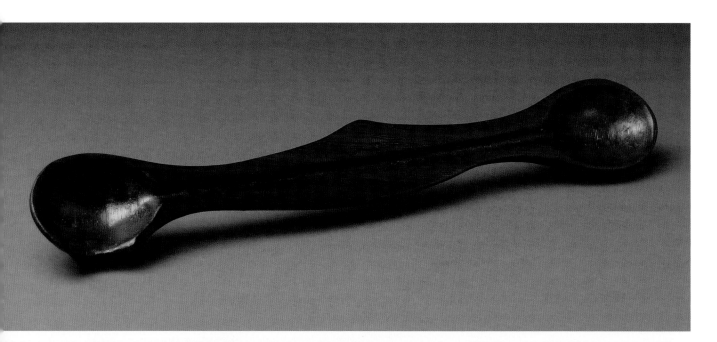

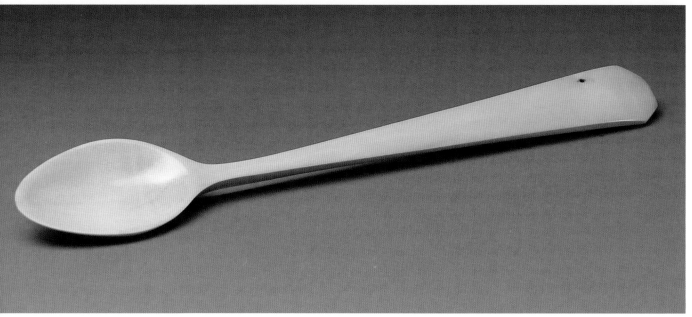

TOP:

Joseph Chasnoff
West Virginia
2010
Bamboo

ABOVE:

Russ Cherry
Alabama
2006
Privet

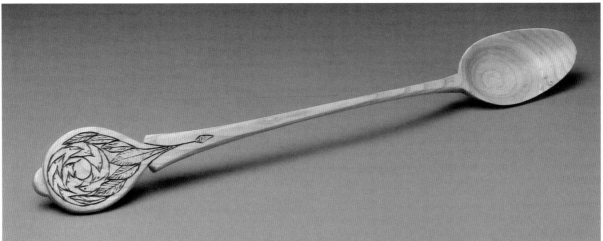

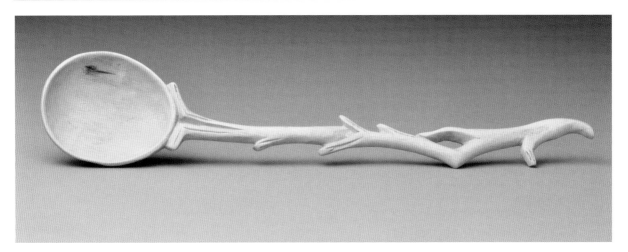

TOP:

John Chesnes
Connecticut
2009
White birch

MIDDLE:

Dennis Chicolte
Minnesota
2009
Pin cherry

ABOVE:

Wilber Ciprian
Peru
2011
Tara

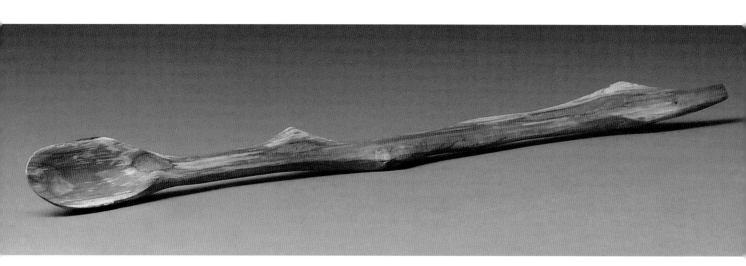

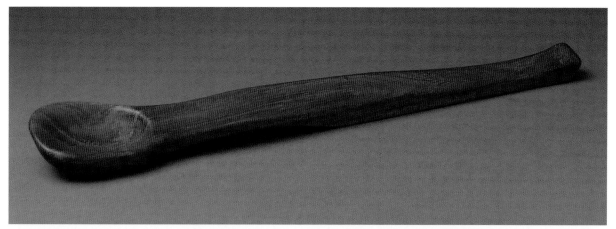

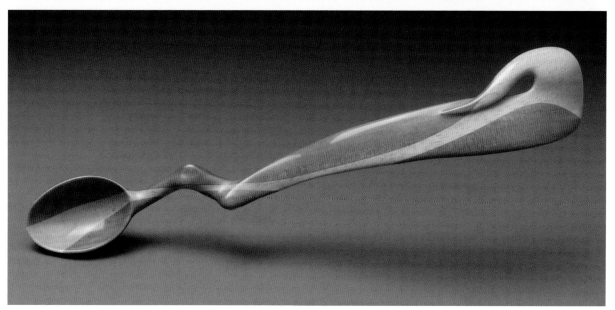

TOP:

Aaron Clapp
New Hampshire
2011
Rose

MIDDLE:

Perry Cobb
New York
2006
Osage orange

ABOVE:

Ray Cologon
Australia
2006
Southern myrtle,
silver ash

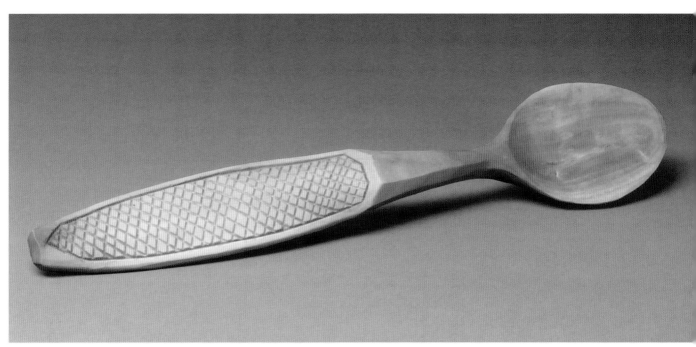

TOP:

Matthew Comer
North Carolina
2010
Bradford pear

ABOVE AND RIGHT:

Ron Cook
California
2006
Flowering plum

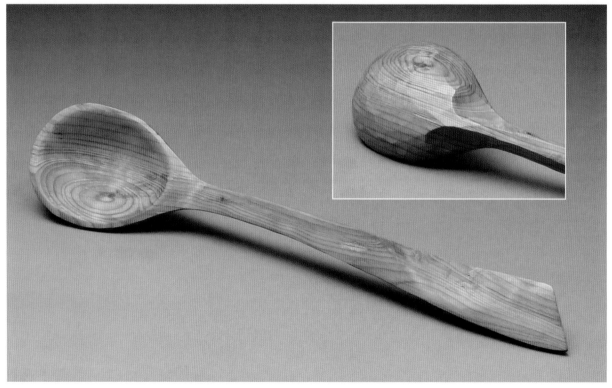

TOP:

Jeffrey Cooper
New Jersey
2006
Jatoba

ABOVE:

William Coperthwaite
Maine
2006
Yew

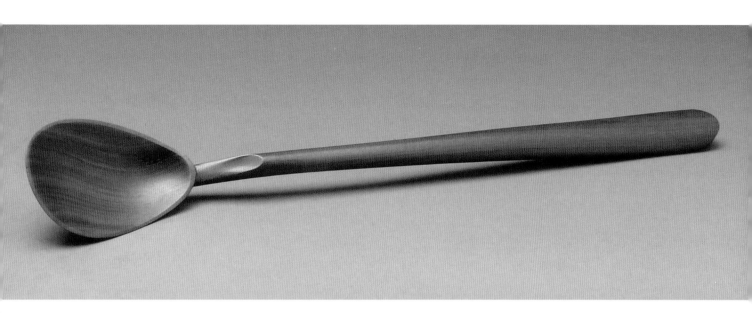

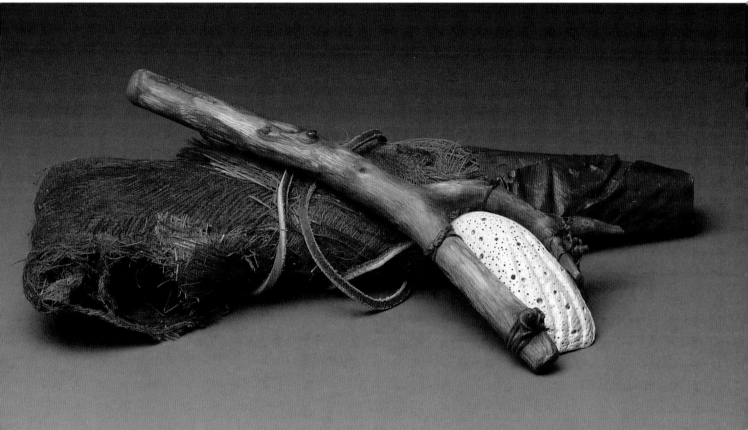

TOP:
Martin Corbin
Australia
2007
Western myall

ABOVE:
Rick Crawford
Florida
2011
Sugar maple (bowl),
black mangrove

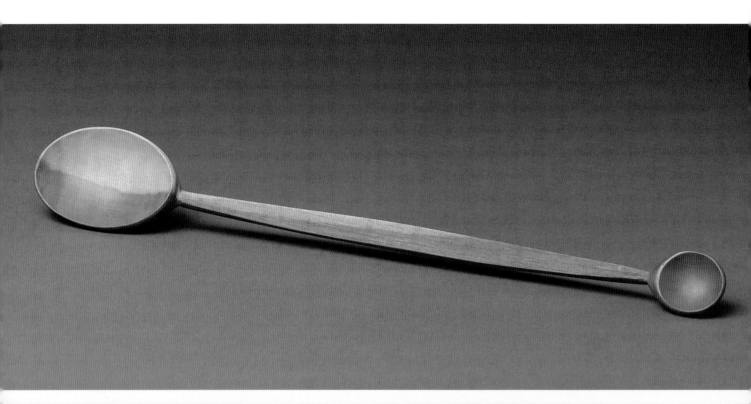

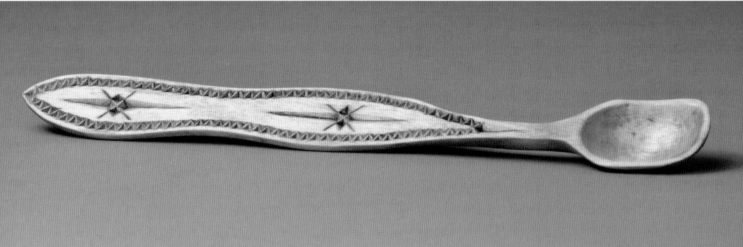

TOP:

Michael Cullen
California
2010
Mountain mahogany

ABOVE:

Sam Culp
Missouri
2012
Maple

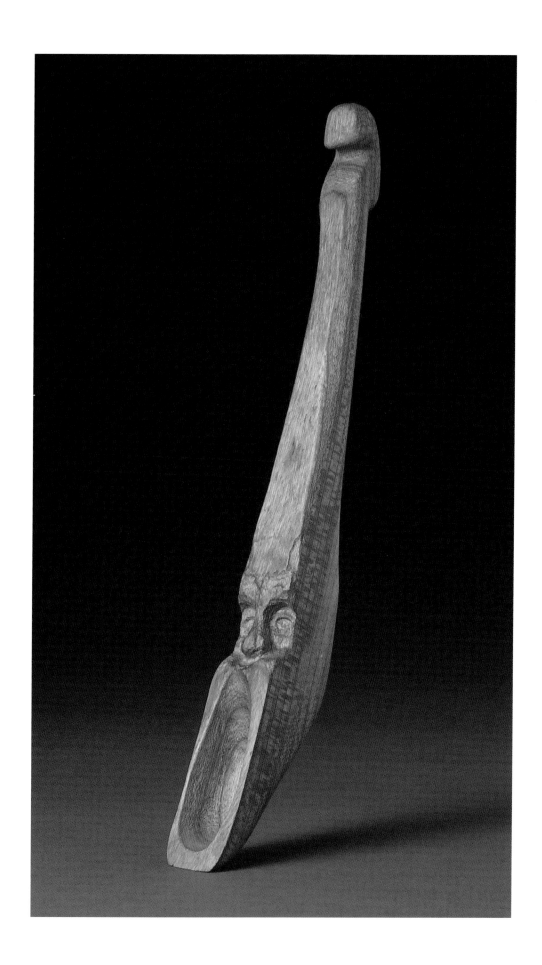

Liviu Cupceancu
Connecticut
2011
Cherry

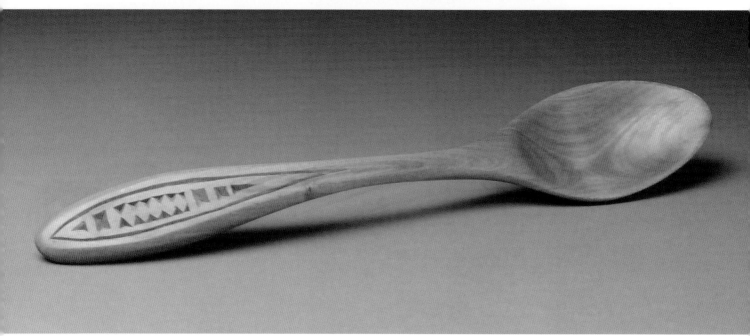

TOP:

Jeff Cupp
Alabama
2010
Sparkleberry

ABOVE:

Jarrod Dahl
Wisconsin
2009
Buckthorn

TOP:

Martin Damen
England
2011
Cherry plum

ABOVE:

George Darwall
England
2011
Boxwood

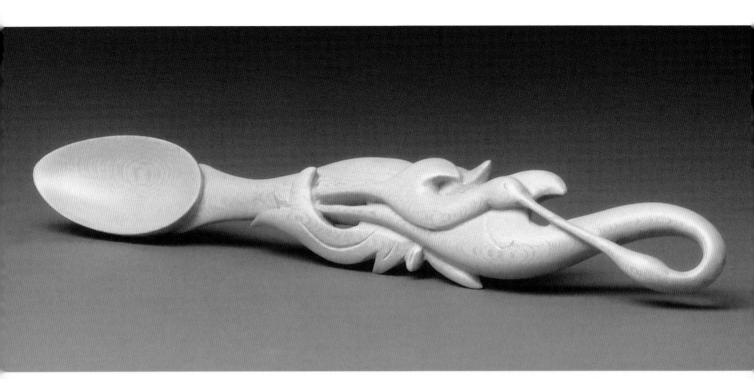

TOP:

Mike Davies
Wales
2010
Lime

ABOVE:

Karen Davis
Tennessee
2007
White oak

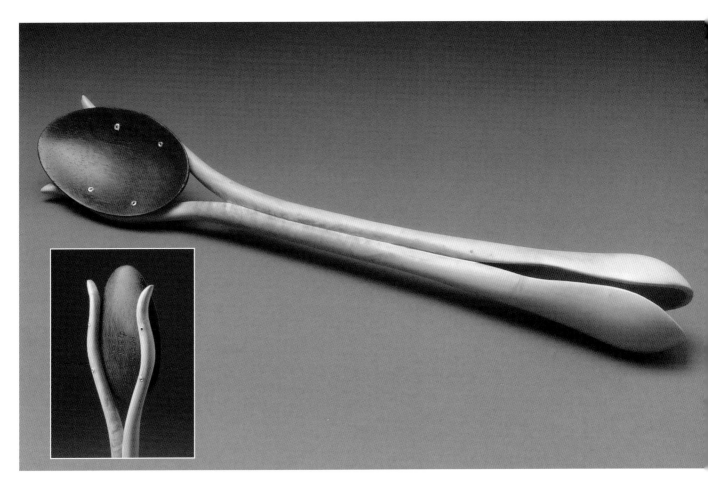

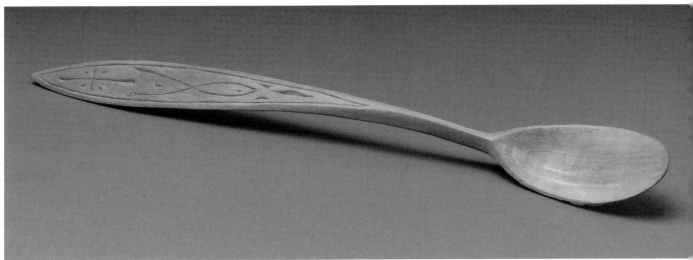

TOP:

Jon Delp
Virginia
2008
English boxwood,
purpleheart

ABOVE:

Tom Dengler
Minnesota
2008
Birch

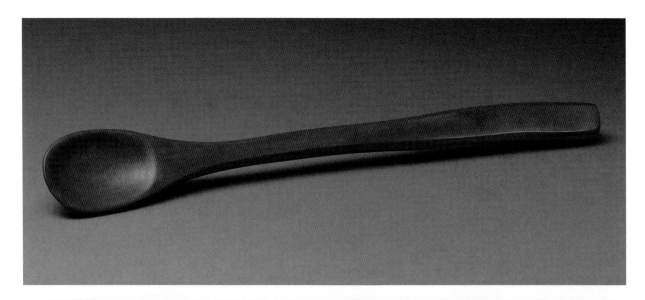

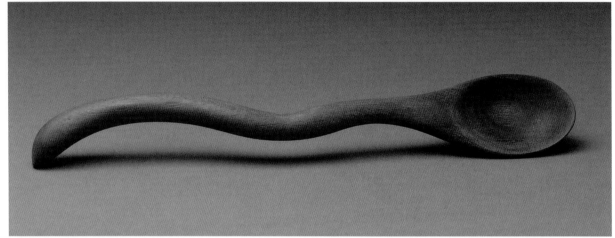

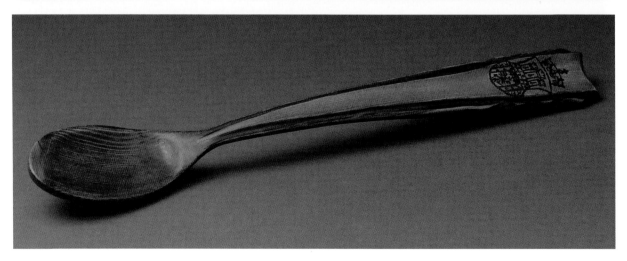

TOP:	MIDDLE:	ABOVE:
Bob DeWitt	Skip Dewhirst	Matthew Domiczek
Pennsylvania	Vermont	Connecticut
2006	2006	2009
Cherry	Pilon	Unidentified

BELOW:

Dan Dustin
New Hampshire
2006
Blueberry

RIGHT:

Kelly Dunn
Hawaii
2010
Lama

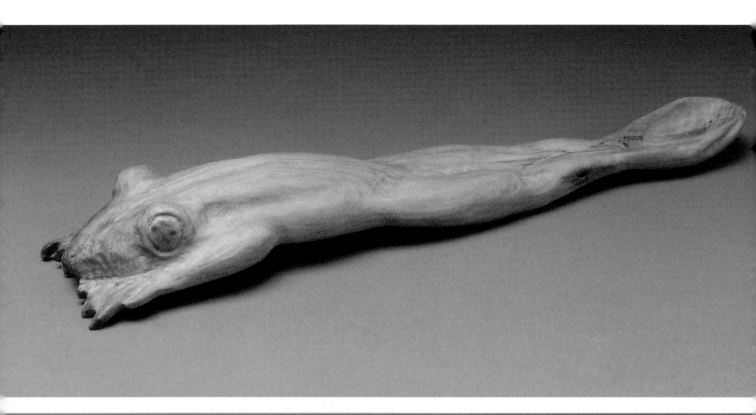

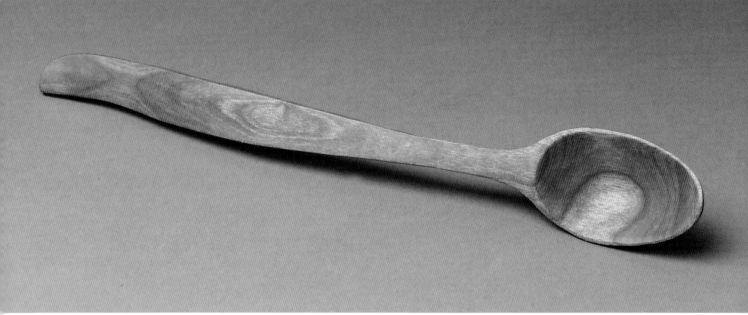

TOP:

Mark English
West Virginia
2008
White oak

ABOVE:

Ryland Erdman
Wisconsin
2009
Lilac

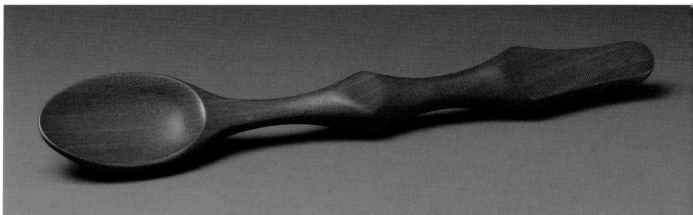

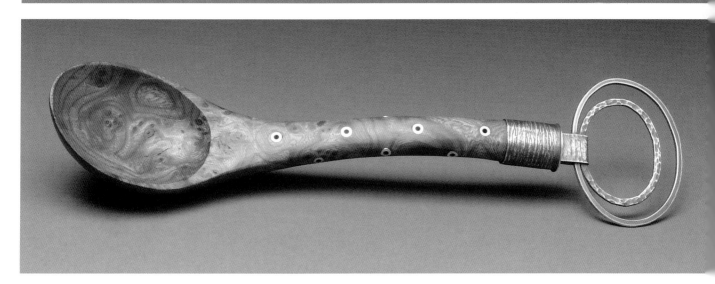

TOP:
Hassan Ezzaki
Morocco
2011
Juniper

MIDDLE:
Peter Faletra
New Hampshire
2006
Cherry

ABOVE:
Deb Fanelli
Vermont
2008
Danish elm

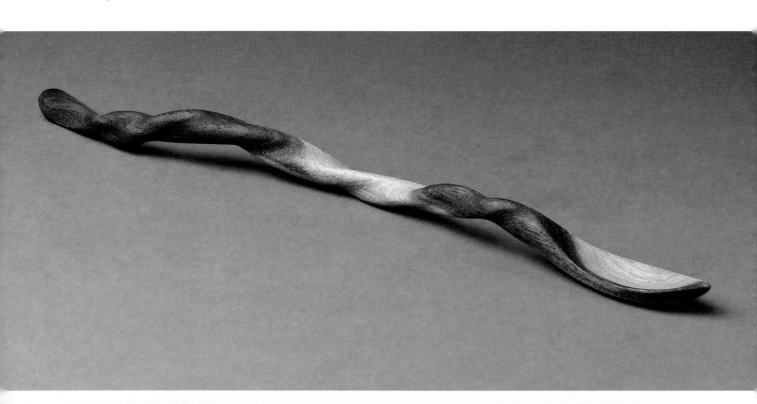

TOP:

Rich Fasel
Texas
2010
Texas ebony

ABOVE:

Robin Fawcett
England
2011
Laburnum

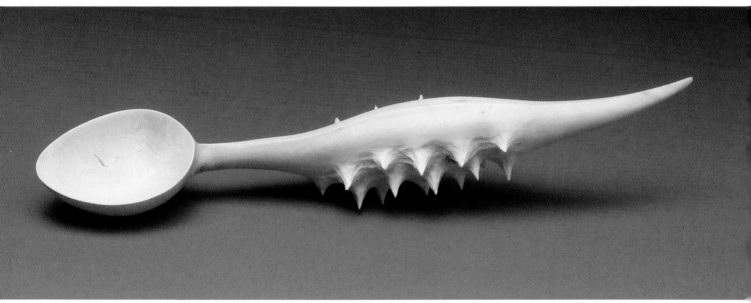

TOP:
Roger Filipelli
California
2007
Manzinita

ABOVE:
Doug Finkel
Virginia
2008
Boxwood

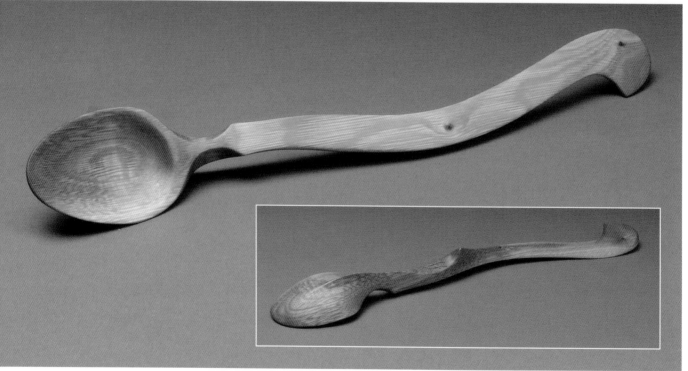

TOP:

Eddie Fletcher
West Virginia
2006
Sugar maple

ABOVE:

Frank Foltz
Minnesota
2006
Buckthorn

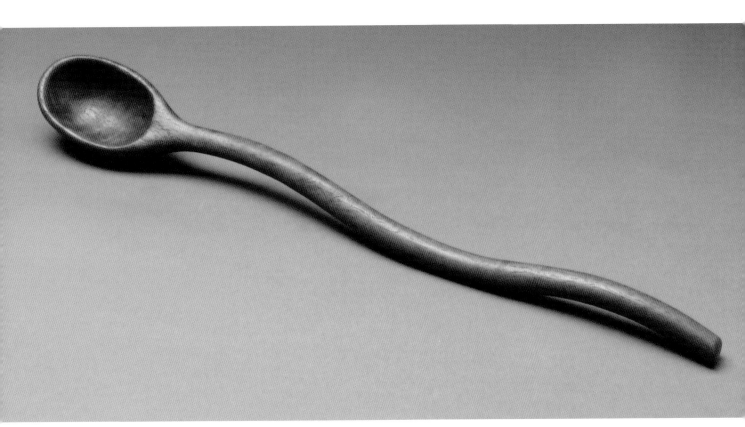

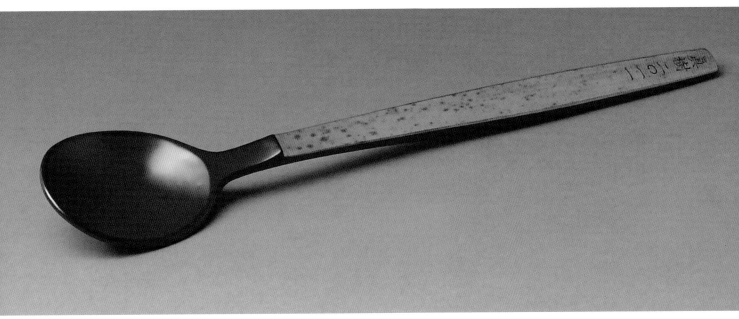

TOP:

Ken Free
Australia
2006
Red gum

ABOVE:

Maki Fushimi
Japan
2011
Bamboo

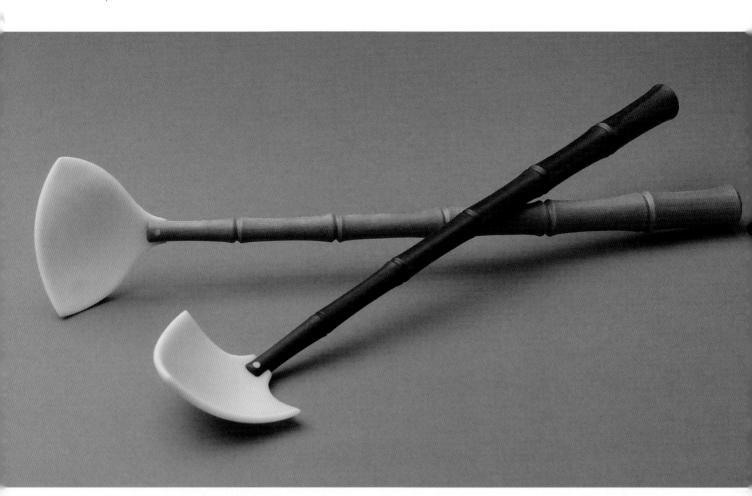

TOP:

Mark Gardner
North Carolina
2006
Dogwood,
ebony, tagua

ABOVE:

Dewey Garrett
California
2010
Walnut

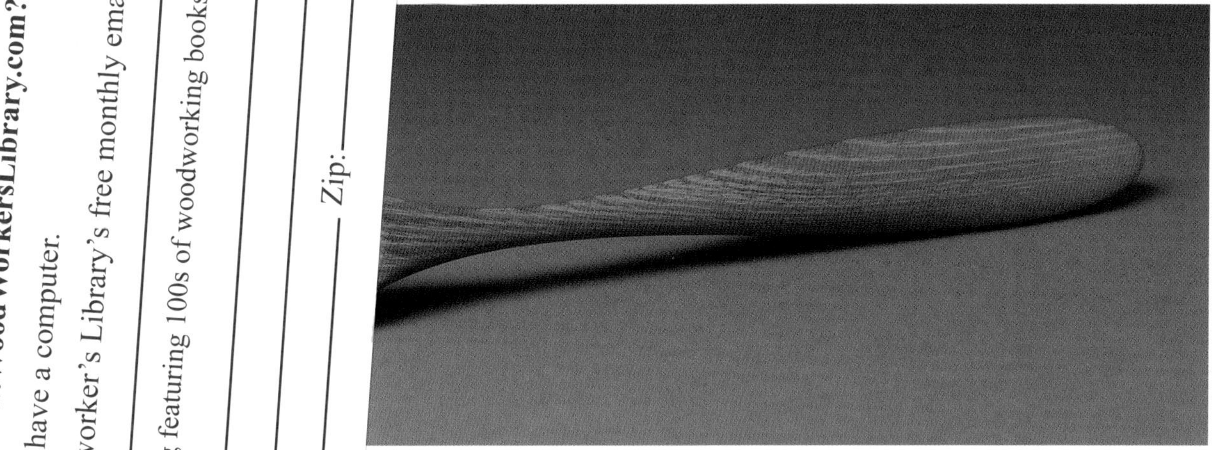

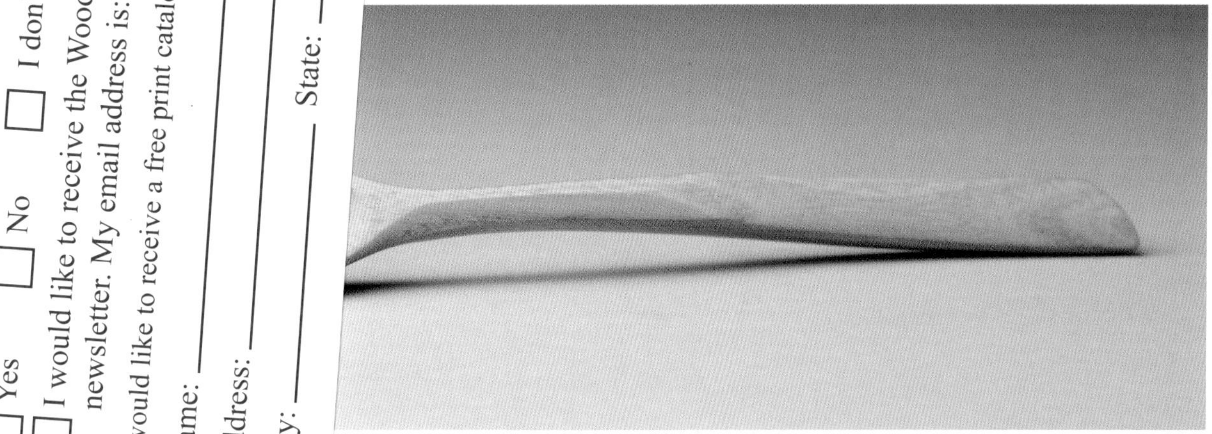

ABOVE:

Mike Glasgow
Alaska
2006
Purpleheart

Steve Gobic
Tennessee
2010
Osage orange

Barry Gordon
New York
2011
Elm

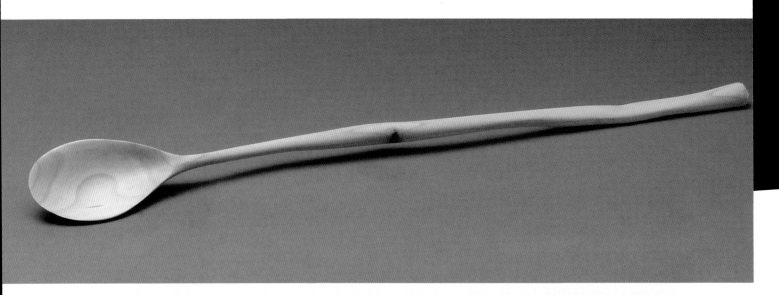

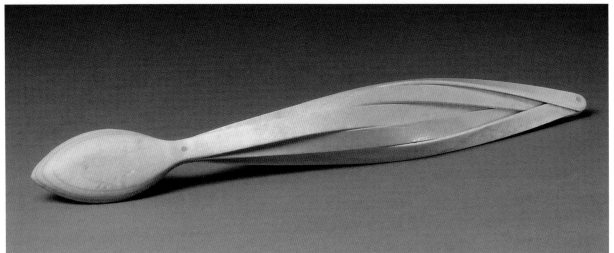

TOP:

Rick Gorman
California
2006
Santa Rosa plum

MIDDLE:

Hans Gottsacker
Michigan
2011
Maple

ABOVE:

Trevor Hadden
California
2010
Teak

PLACE
POSTAGE
HERE

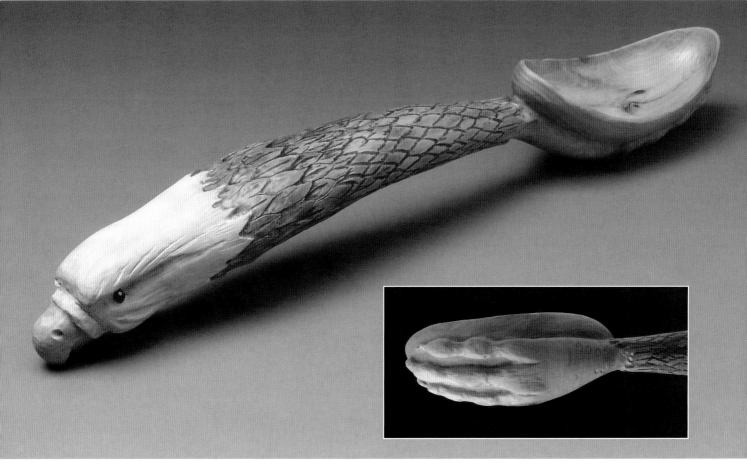

TOP:

David Hanson
Missouri
2008
Cherry

ABOVE:

Connie Hardt
Arkansas
2006
Madrone

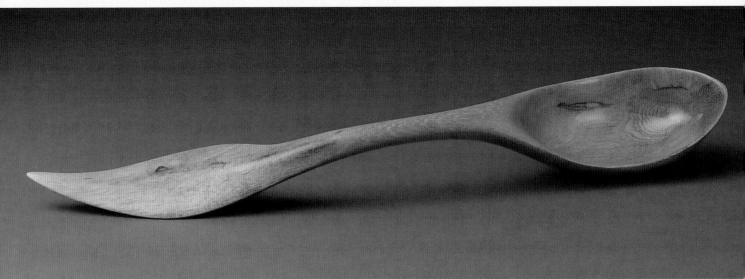

TOP:

Jan Harm der Brugge
Netherlands
2006
Birch

ABOVE:

Helen Harrison
Florida
2010
Bougainvillea

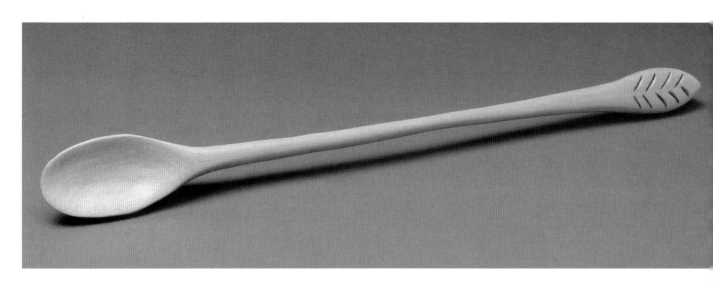

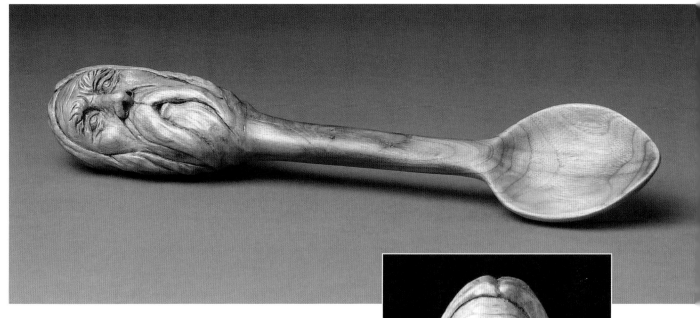

TOP:

Ray Helgager
South Dakota
2006
Birch

ABOVE AND RIGHT:

Johnny Hembree
North Carolina
2007
Spalted butternut

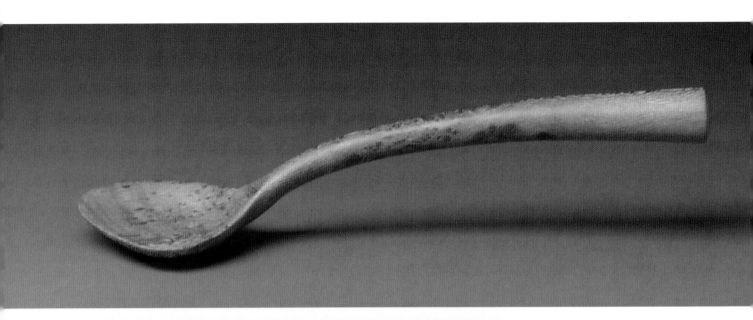

ABOVE:
Sean Hellman
England
2011
London plane

LEFT:
Ralph Hentall
England
2010
Oak

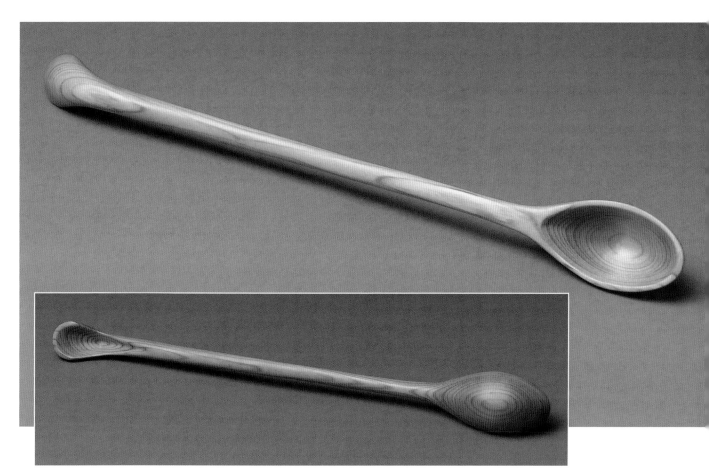

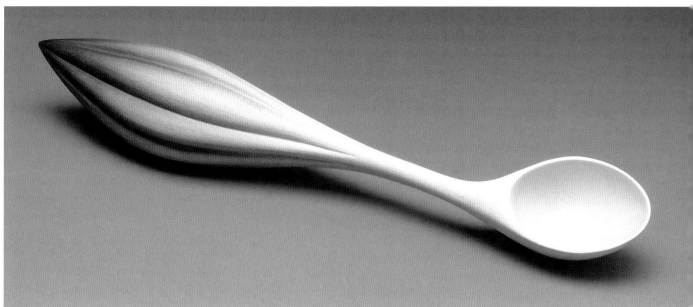

TOP:

Lance Herriott
Canada
2009
Yew

ABOVE:

Louise Hibbert
England
2008
English sycamore

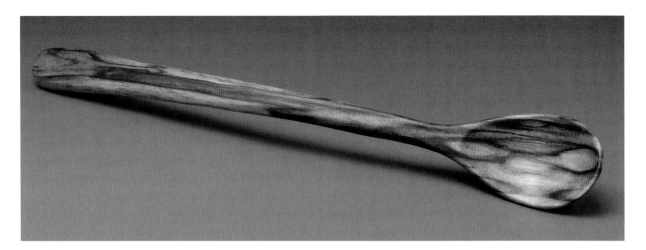

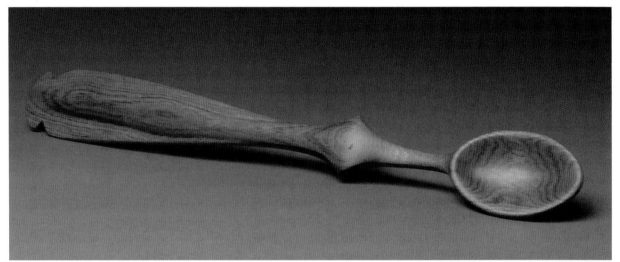

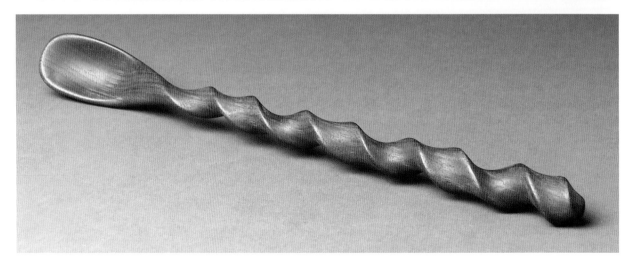

TOP:	MIDDLE:	ABOVE:
Jim Hill	Simon Hill	Rita Hjelle
Montana	England	North Dakota
2008	2011	2008
Spalted birch	Laburnum	Black walnut

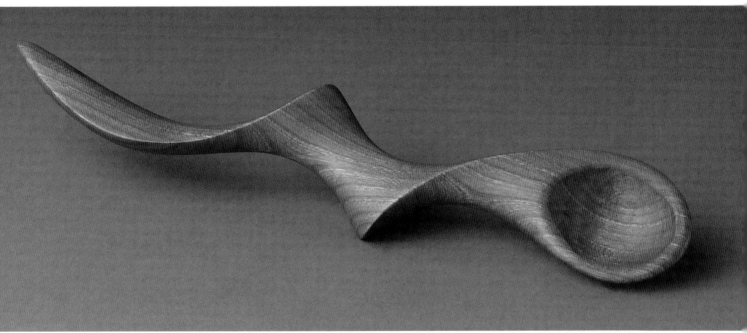

TOP:
Rodney Hopkins
North Carolina
2009
American holly

ABOVE:
David Hurwitz
Vermont
2007
Cherry

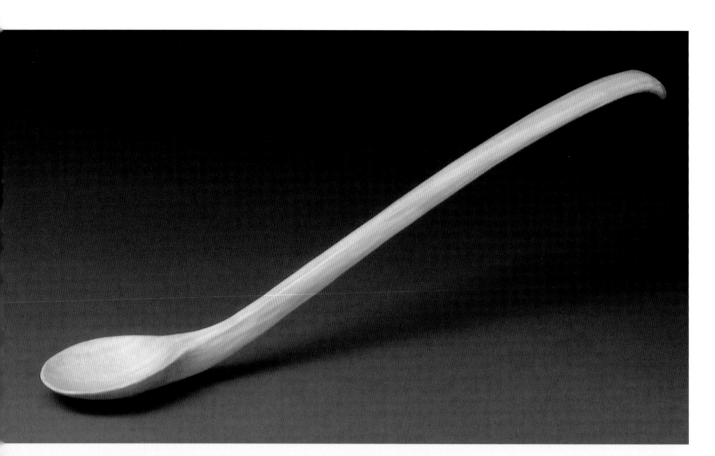

TOP:

Tomio Imaru
Japan
2010
Maple

ABOVE:

Constantin Ion
Romania
2008
Birch

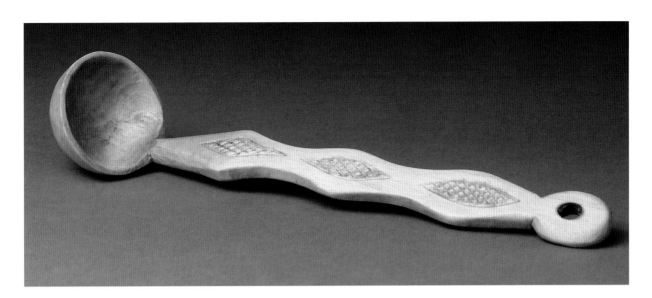

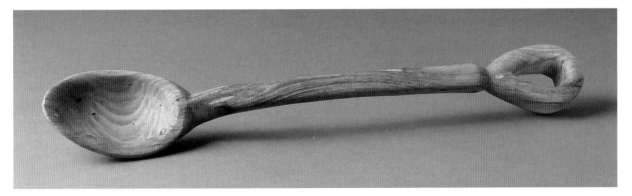

TOP:
Vasile Iremescu
Romania
2008
Elder

MIDDLE:
Noriko Isogai
Vermont
2011
Catalpa

ABOVE:
Sue Jennings
West Virginia
2010
Poison ivy

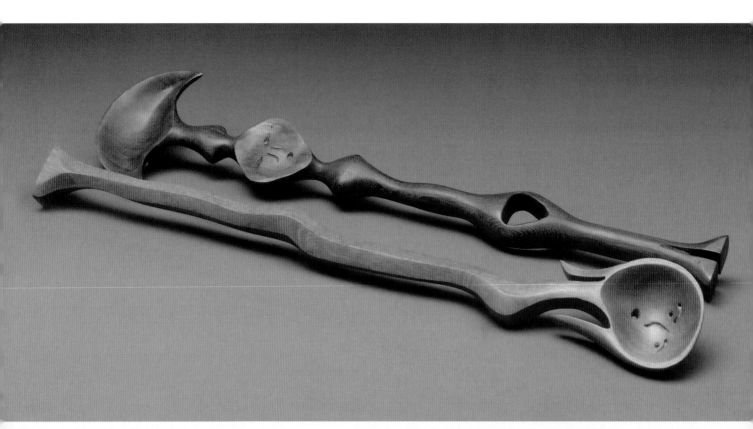

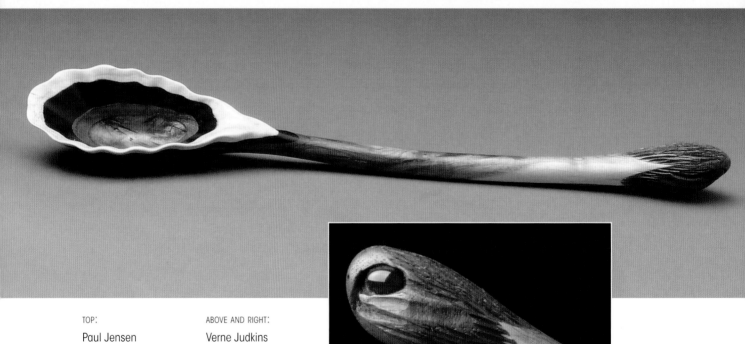

TOP:

Paul Jensen
Wisconsin
2007
Brown ebony,
pink ivory

ABOVE AND RIGHT:

Verne Judkins
Idaho
2007
Ebony, plum,
walnut, bone

ABOVE AND LEFT:

Anatolyi Kalinka
Lithuania
2008
Birch

TOP:

Phil Jurus
Pennsylvania
2010
Maple

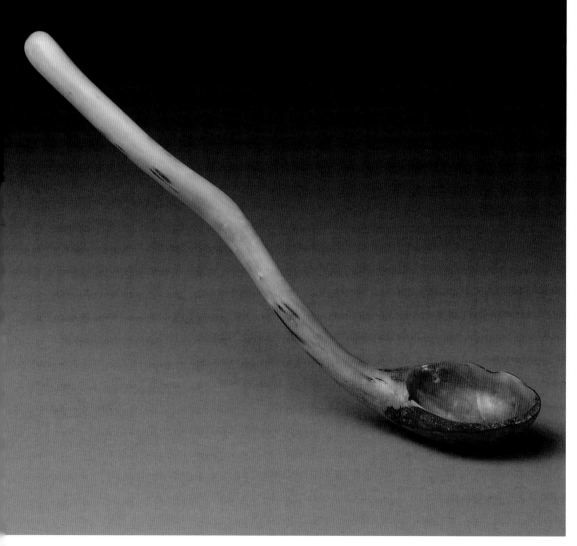

ABOVE:

Henry Karlsson
Sweden
2005
Plum

LEFT:

Beth Kenyon
Ohio
2007
Rhododendron

ABOVE:

Rich Klein
South Carolina
2006
Spalted pink
dogwood

RIGHT:

Wladek Klusiewicz
Poland
2008
Linden

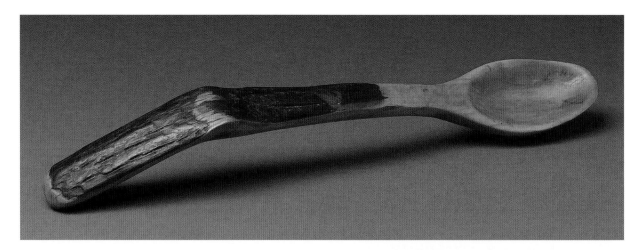

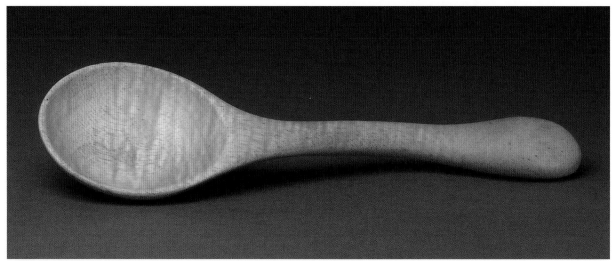

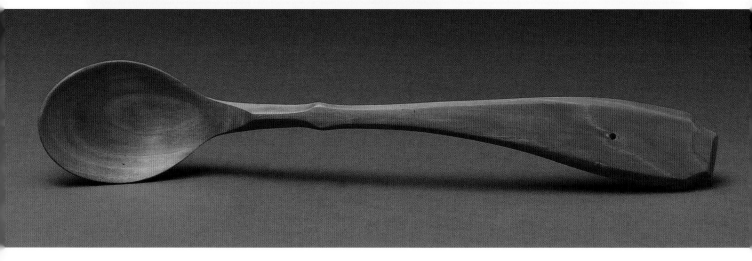

TOP:

Mark Kneeland
New Hampshire
2006
Laurel

MIDDLE:

Michael Koren
Australia
2011
Silver ash

ABOVE:

Emma Kromvic School carvers
Minnesota
2007
Apricot

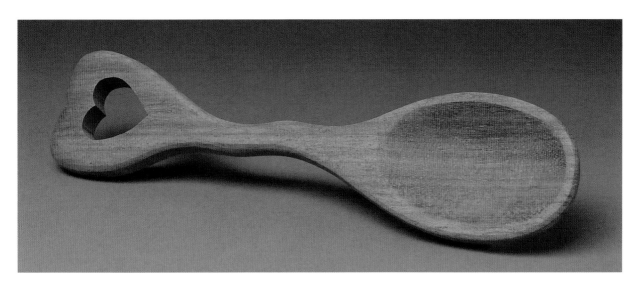

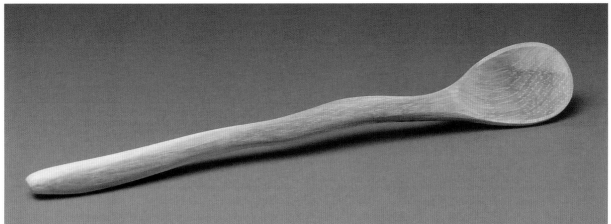

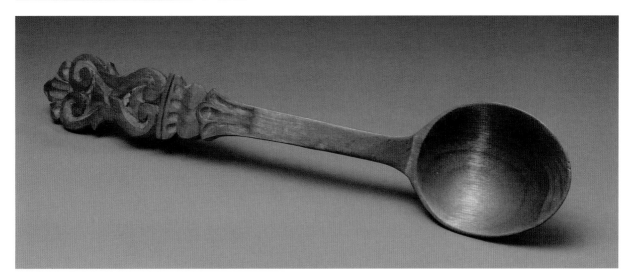

TOP:	MIDDLE:	ABOVE:
Jim & Karen Kuhlmann	Simon Lamb	Tom Latané
Texas	England	Wisconsin
2006	2011	2008
Cherry	Beech	Birch

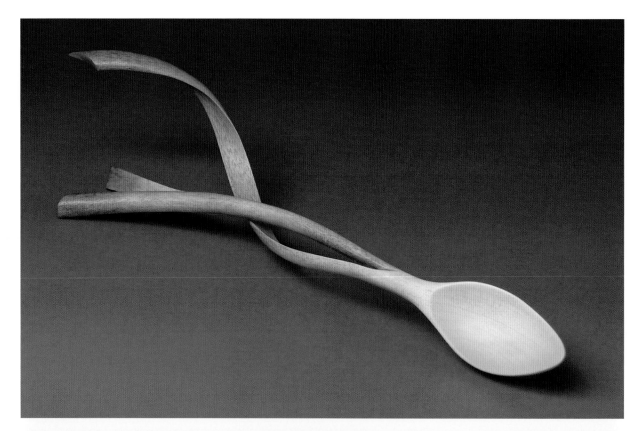

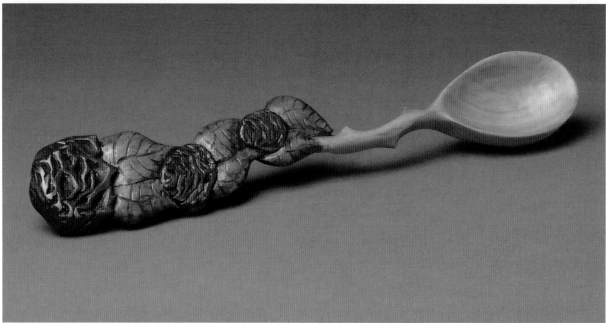

TOP:

Kristin LeVier
Idaho
2011
Compressed maple

ABOVE:

Phil Lingelbach
Oregon
2010
Cascara

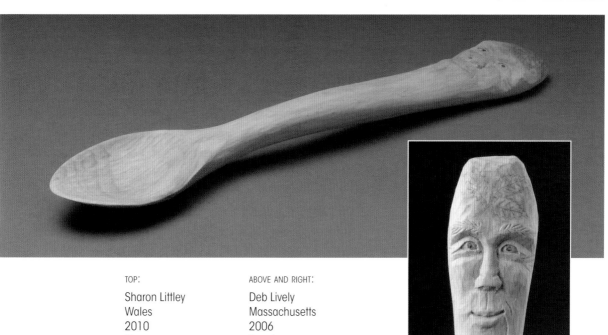

TOP:

Sharon Littley
Wales
2010
Plum

ABOVE AND RIGHT:

Deb Lively
Massachusetts
2006
Beech

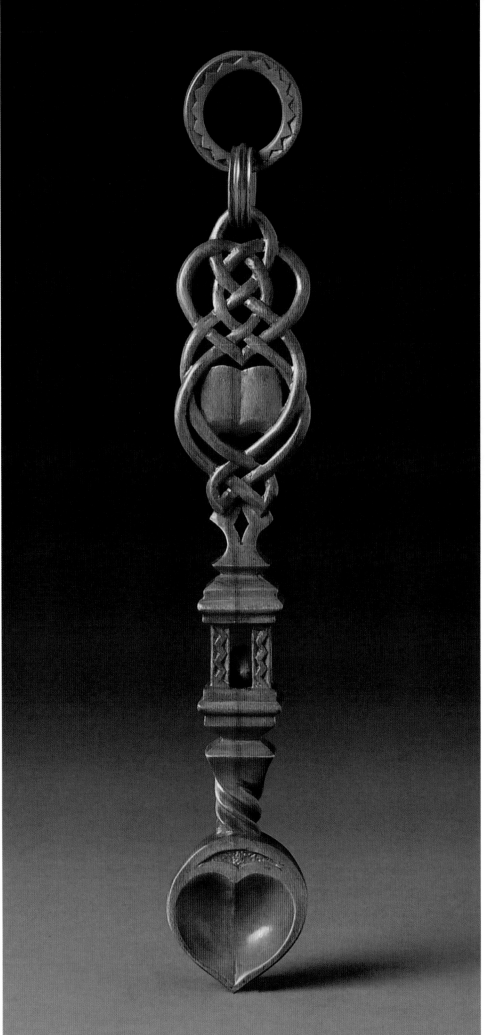

Siôn Llewellyn
Wales
2010
Holly

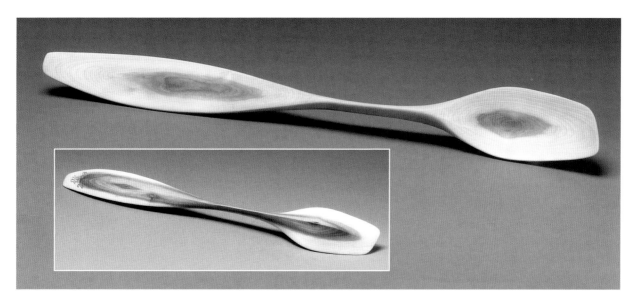

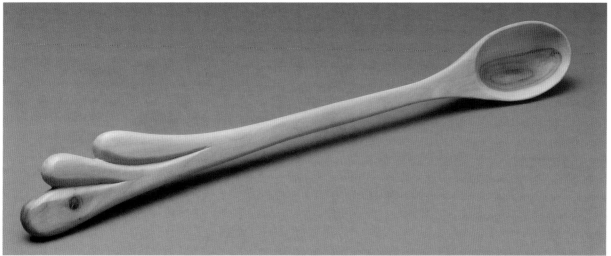

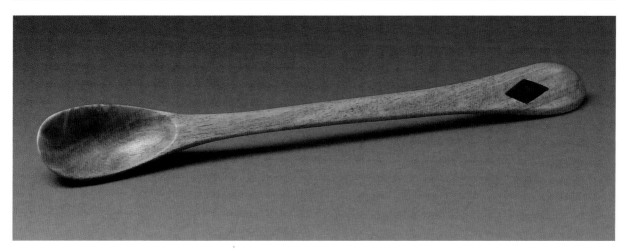

TOP:
Fred Livesay
Minnesota
2010
Lilac

MIDDLE:
Barry Loewen
Canada
2006
Apple

ABOVE:
Clifford Lee Logan
Michigan
2006
Orange

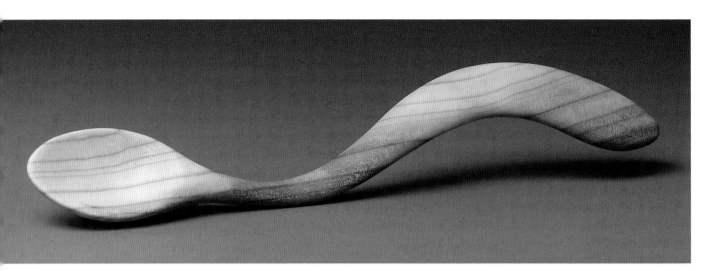

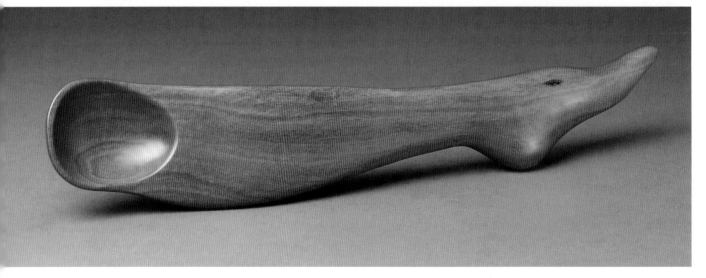

TOP:

Tom Lowe
Virginia
2008
Magnolia

MIDDLE:

Becky Lusk
Wisconsin
2009
Butternut

ABOVE:

Marty Mandelbaum
New York
2010
Pink ivory

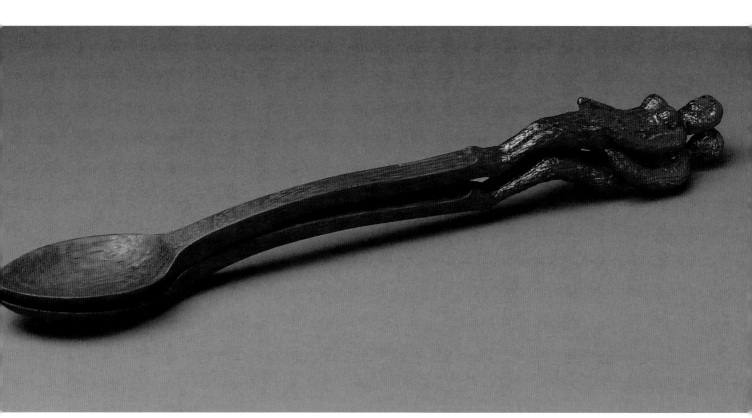

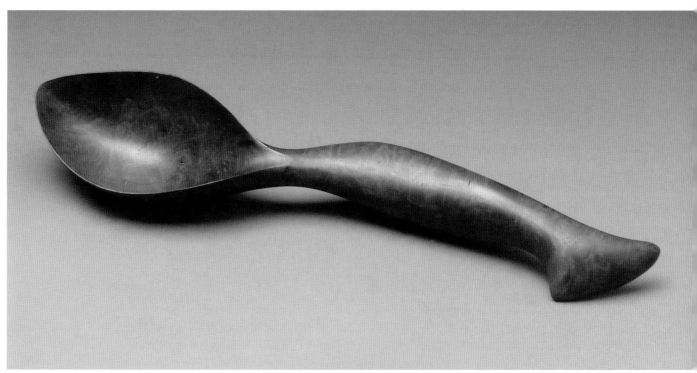

TOP:

John Magnan
Massachusetts
2006
Purpleheart

ABOVE:

Harry Mangalan
California
2007
Ash, black epoxy

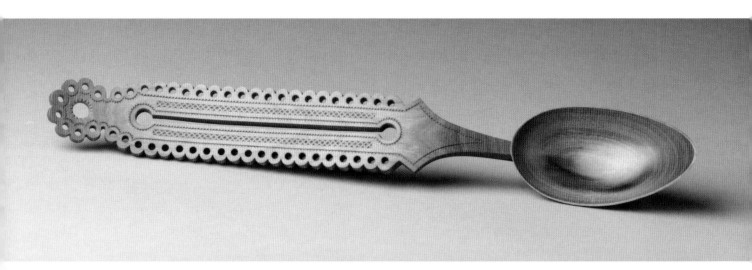

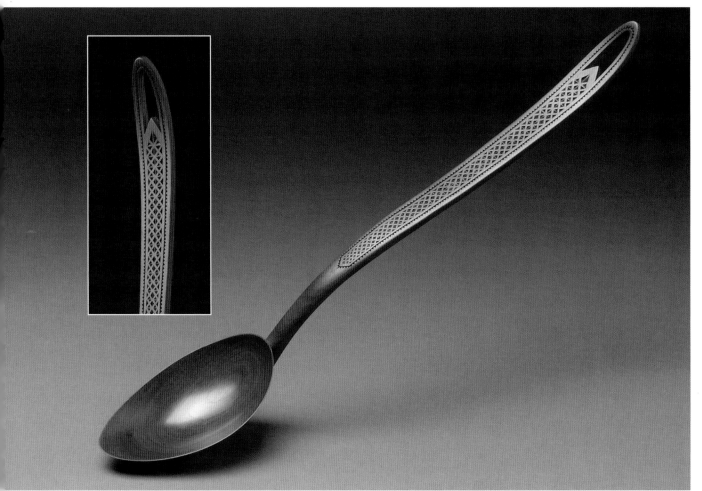

TOP:

Sorin & Zina
Manesa-Burloiu
Romania
2011
Plum

ABOVE:

Zina Manesa-Burloiu
Romania
2008
Plum

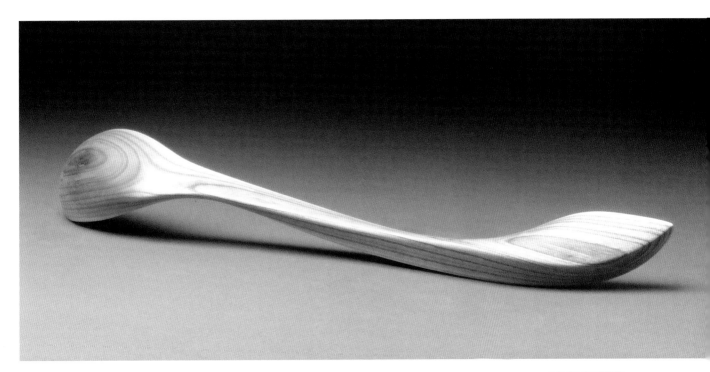

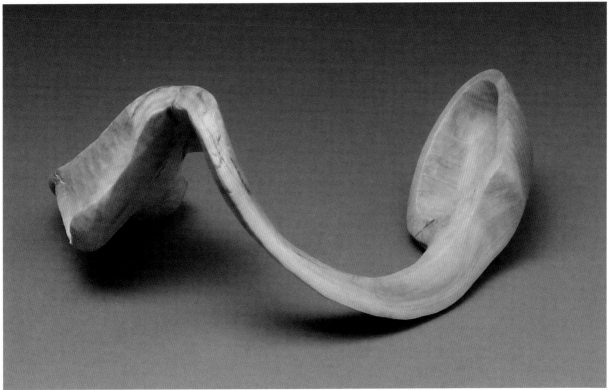

TOP:

Ben Manns
Pennsylvania
2008
Sumac

ABOVE:

Philip Marshall
Alaska
2009
Black spruce

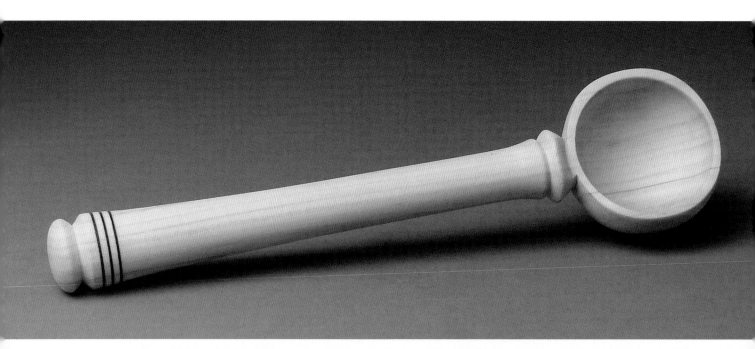

TOP:

Stephen Massman
Missouri
2010
Tulip poplar

ABOVE:

Jim Mayes
California
2011
Yellowheart

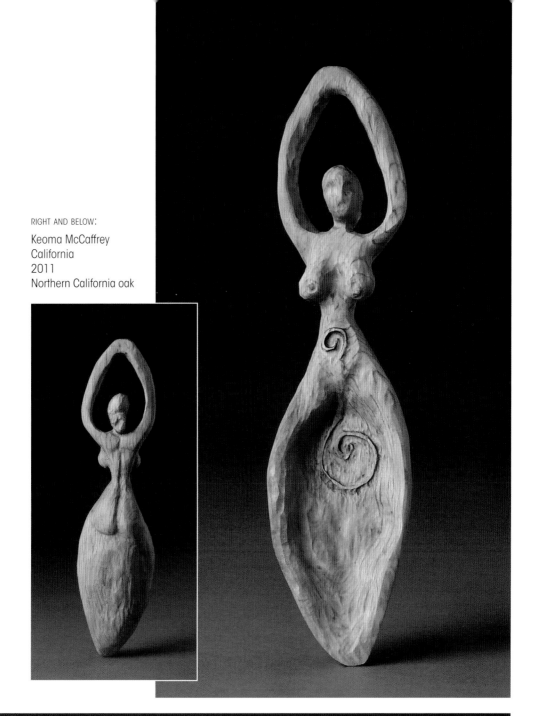

RIGHT AND BELOW:

Keoma McCaffrey
California
2011
Northern California oak

BELOW:

Tom McColley
West Virginia
2006
Red oak

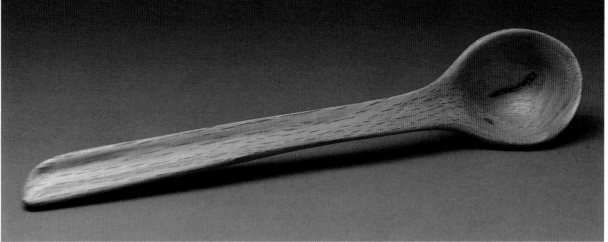

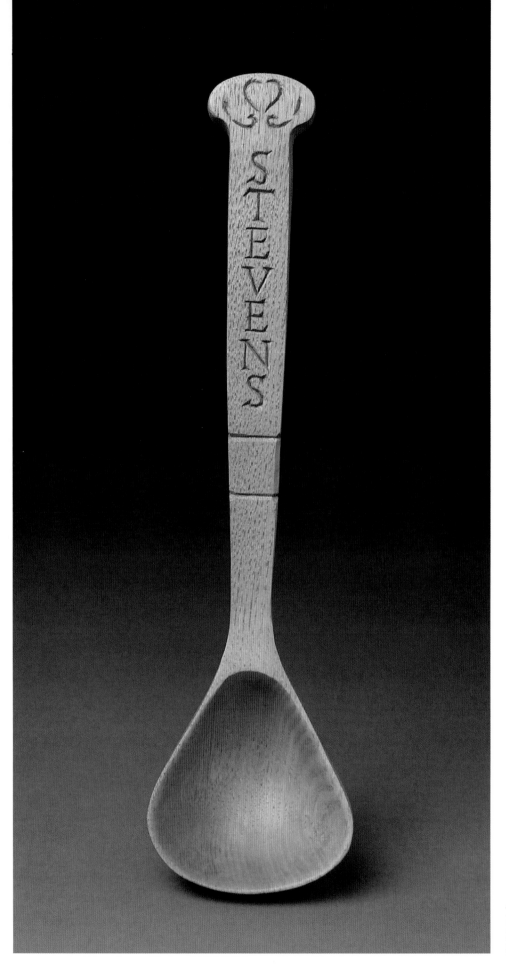

Jim McGie
Tennessee
2006
Sassafras

Richard McHugh
Maine
2010
Sycamore

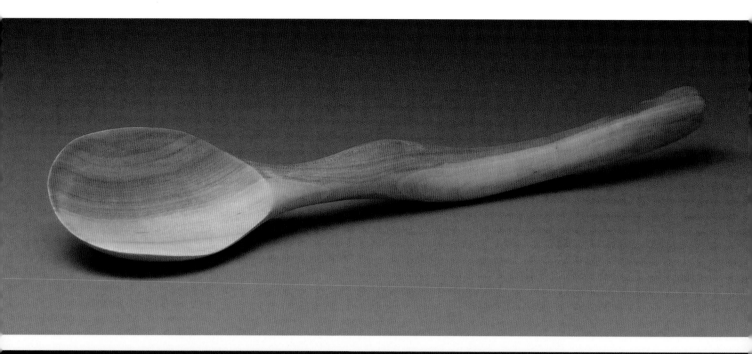

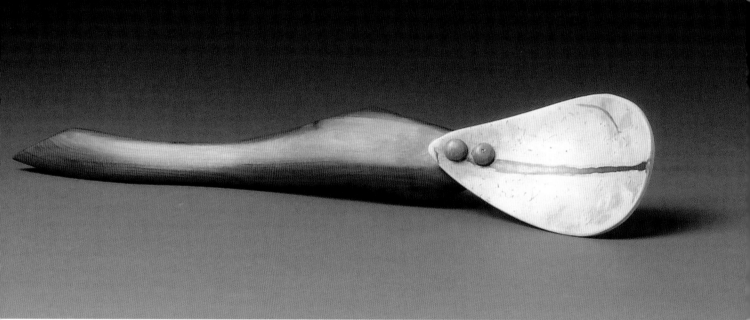

TOP:

Jim McHugh
Massachusetts
2006
Apple

ABOVE:

John McKenzie
Pennsylvania
2011
Cedar, coconut

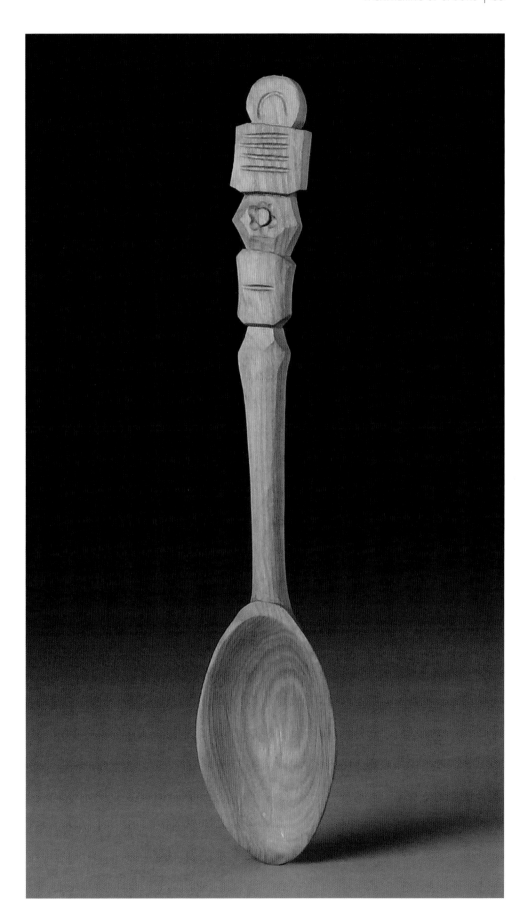

Ray Medeiros
Connecticut
2011
Sweet gum

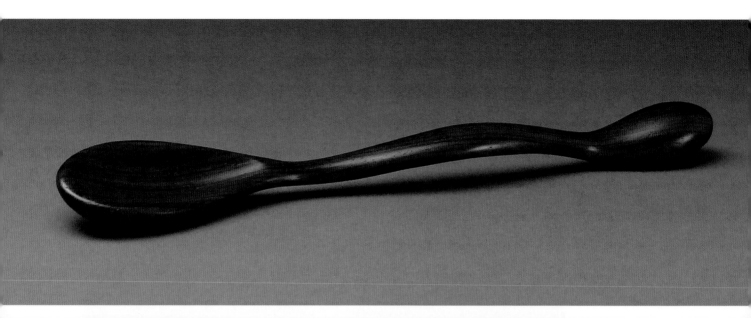

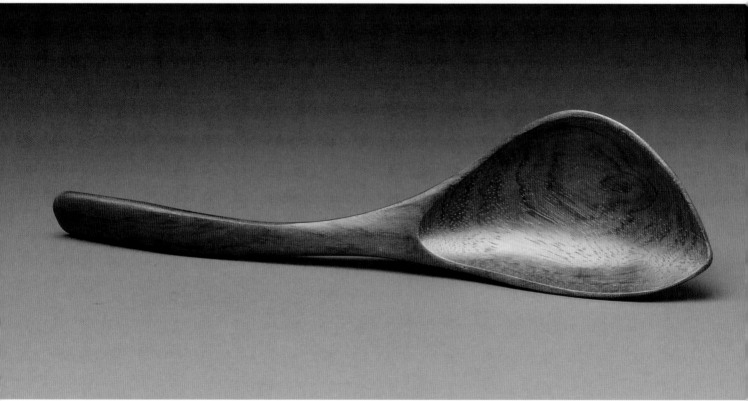

TOP:

Marc Meng
Oklahoma
2006
Cocobolo

ABOVE:

Emil Milan
New Jersey
Undated
Unidentified

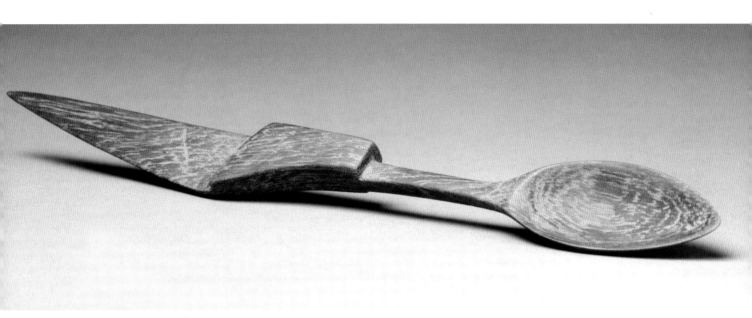

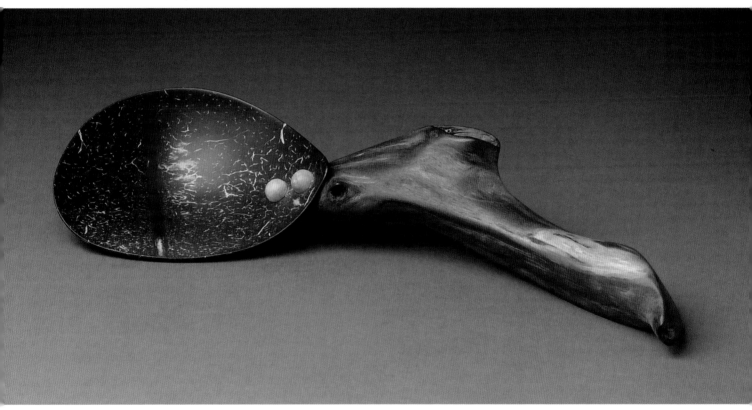

TOP:
Khamis Mnembah
Kenya
2012
Mvule

ABOVE:
Warren Moeller
Bali
2010
Driftwood, coconut

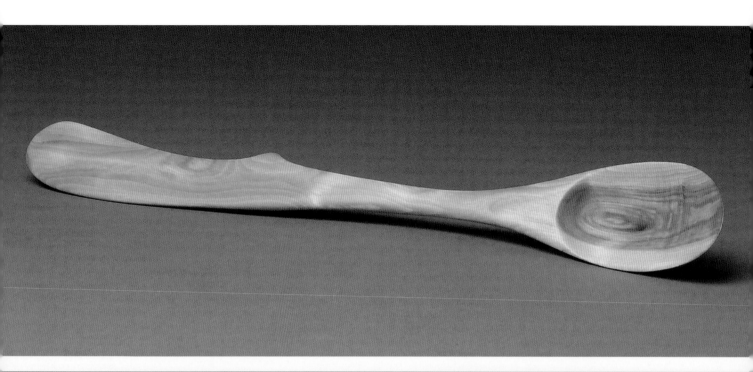

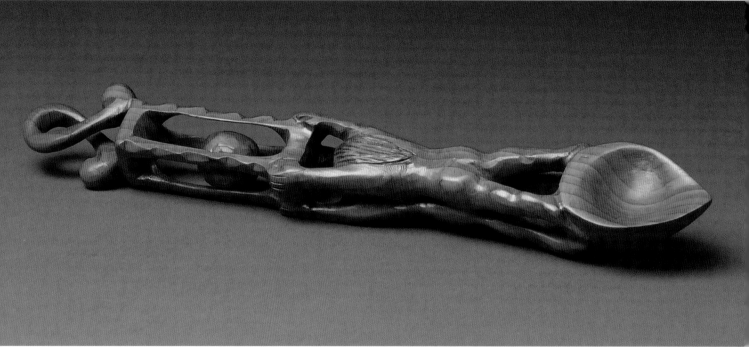

TOP:
Yuri Moldenauer
Minnesota
2011
Lilac

ABOVE:
Andrew Moore
Scotland
2006
Yew

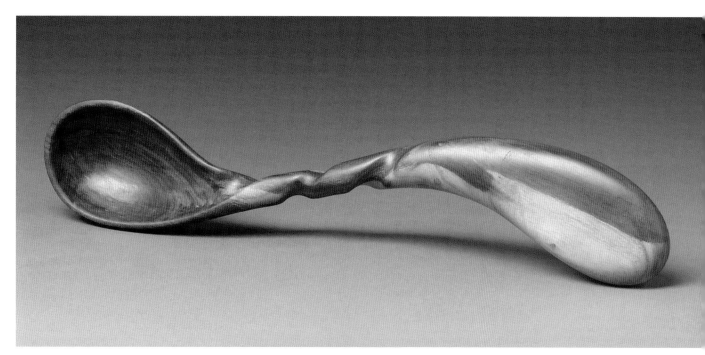

TOP:

John Moore
Washington
2011
Apricot

ABOVE:

Michael Murphy
Kentucky
2011
Kentucky coffee

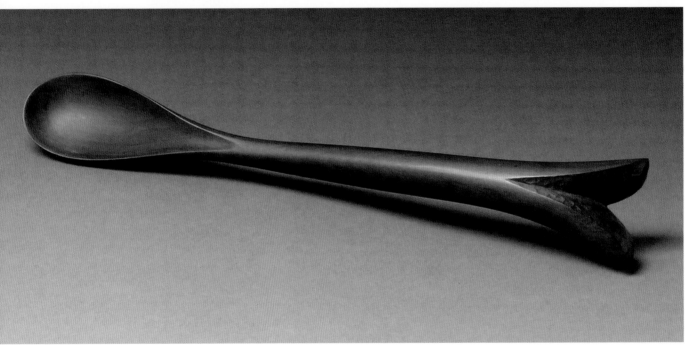

TOP:

Terry Nelson
Texas
2006
Mesquite

ABOVE:

Brian Newell
California
2010
African blackwood

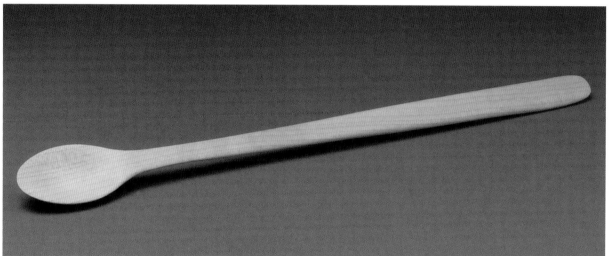

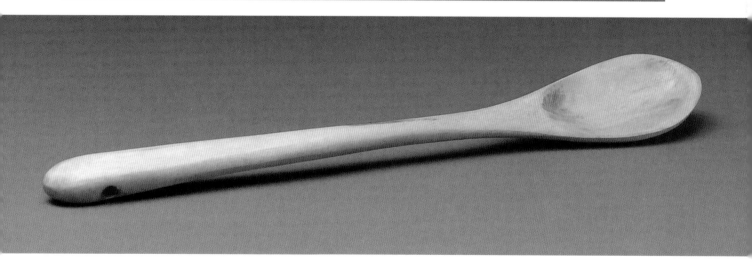

TOP:
M'hamed Nimezouaren
Morocco
2011
Walnut

MIDDLE:
Pascal
Minnesota
2007
Rock maple

ABOVE:
Phil & Joyce Payne
West Virginia
2006
White Birch

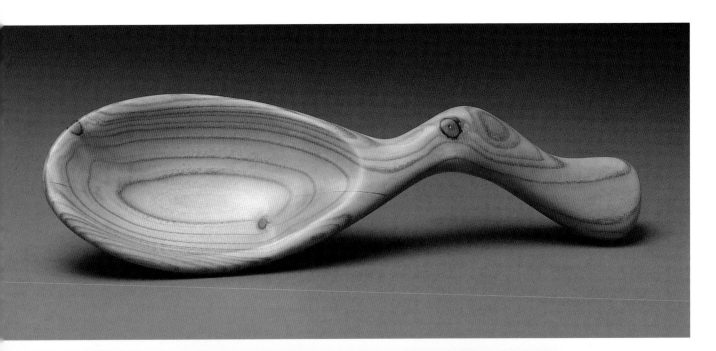

ABOVE:
Peter Petrochko
Connecticut
2011
Pear

LEFT:
Nick Petruska
Alaska
2008
White cedar

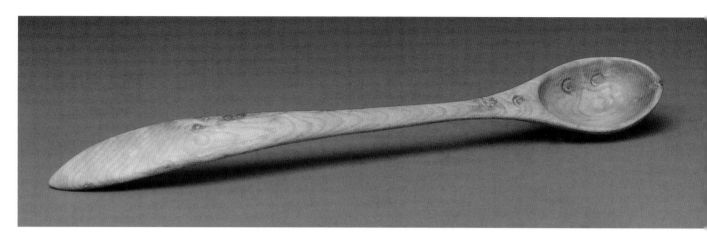

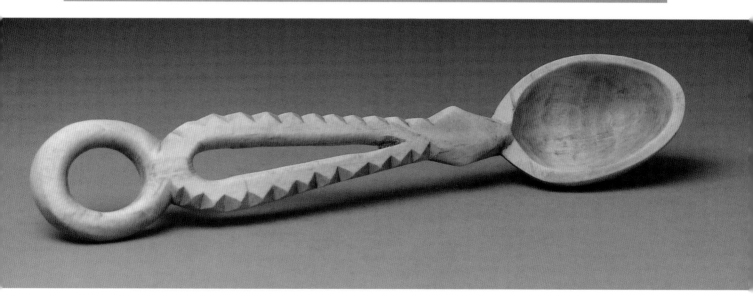

TOP:

Ken Pettigrew
Canada
2007
Birdseye maple

MIDDLE:

Gin Petty
Kentucky
1984
Cherry

ABOVE:

Dragos Puha
Romania
2008
Elder

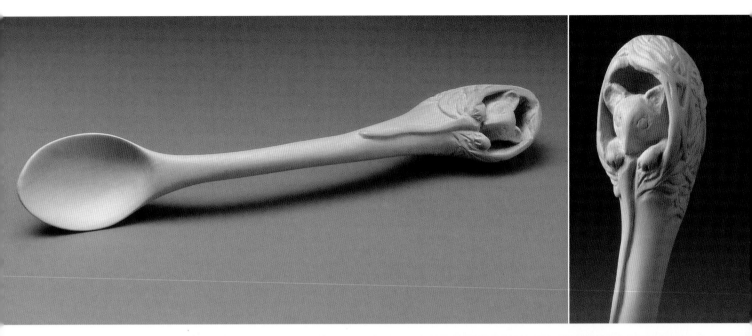

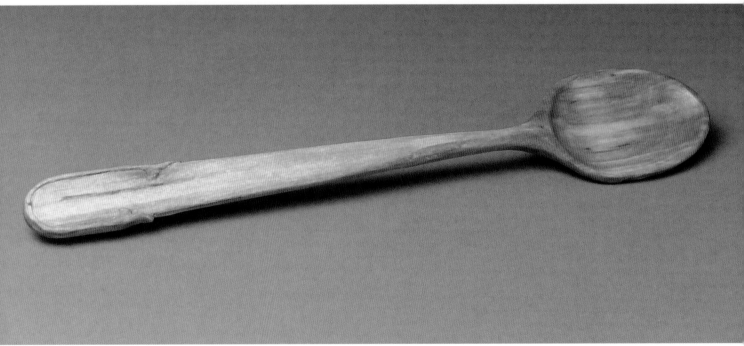

TOP:

Ainslie Pyne
Australia
2008
Huon pine

ABOVE:

Karen Randall
Minnesota
2010
Birch

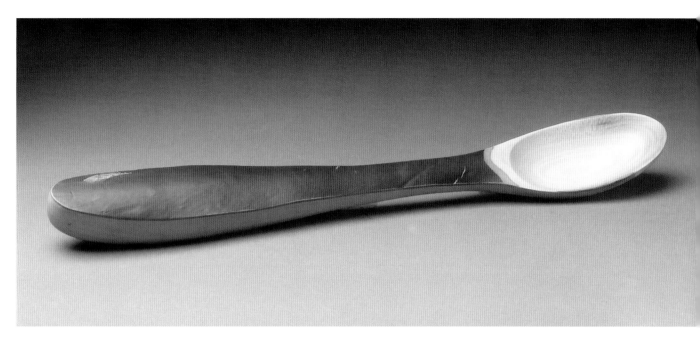

TOP:
Dale Randles
Washington
2006
Madrone

ABOVE:
Judy Ritger
Minnesota
2006
Red cedar

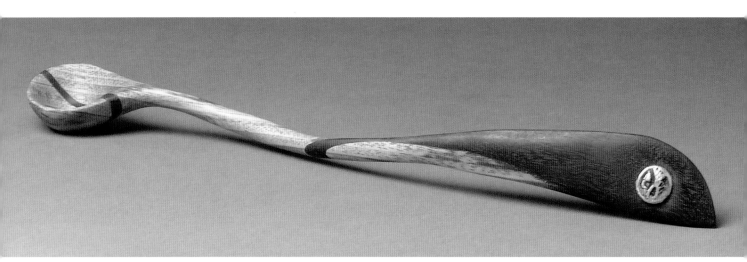

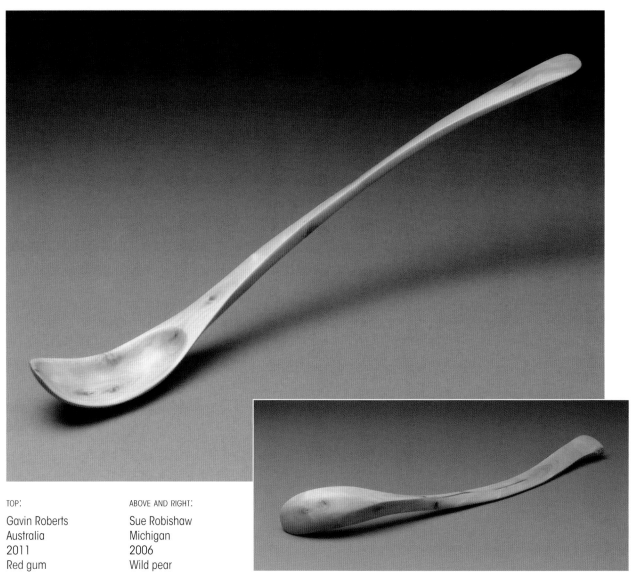

TOP:
Gavin Roberts
Australia
2011
Red gum

ABOVE AND RIGHT:
Sue Robishaw
Michigan
2006
Wild pear

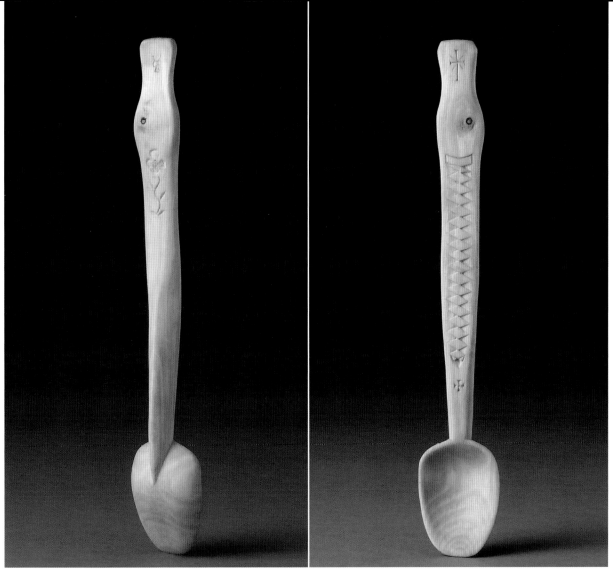

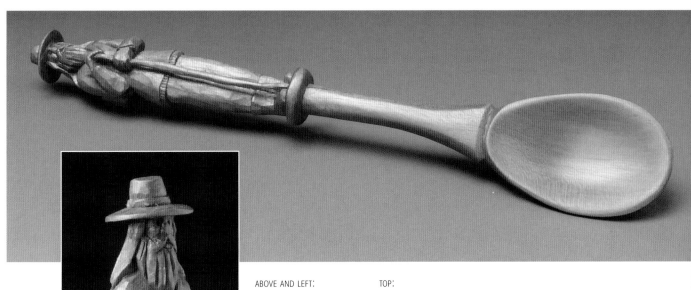

ABOVE AND LEFT:

Dennis Ruane
North Carolina
2007
Cherry

TOP:

Eric Rogers
England
2011
English bird cherry

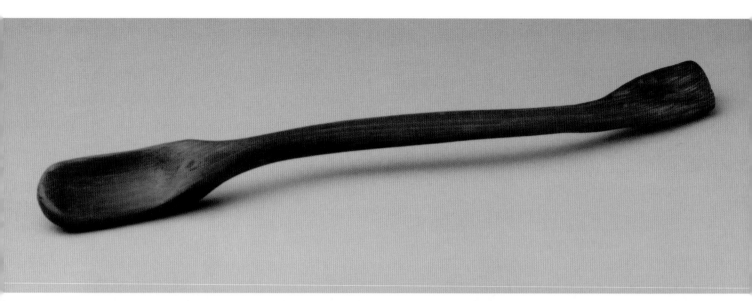

TOP:

Sebastián Ruiz y Pereira
Chile
2012
Alerce

ABOVE:

Jaimie Russell
Canada
2009
Western curly maple

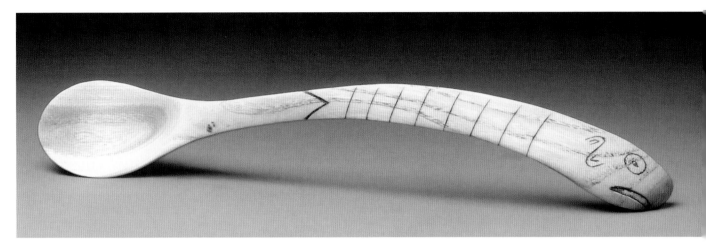

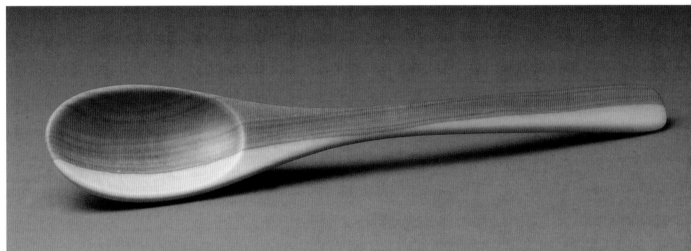

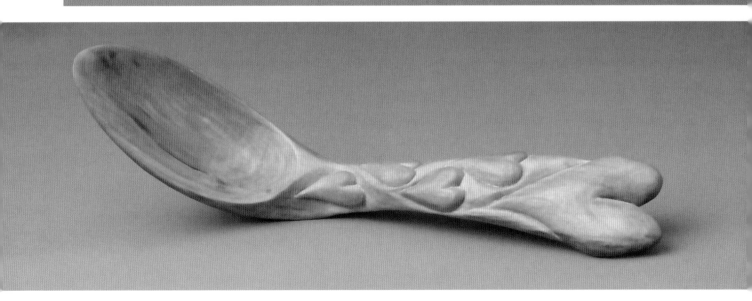

TOP:

Amy Sabrina
Minnesota
2008
Chinese elm

MIDDLE:

Carl Sandstrom
Missouri
2007
Apple

ABOVE:

Jim Sannerud
Minnesota
2010
Birch

TOP:

Stanley Saperstein
New Jersey
2006
Red cedar

ABOVE:

Norm Sartorius
West Virginia
2006
Afzelia lay

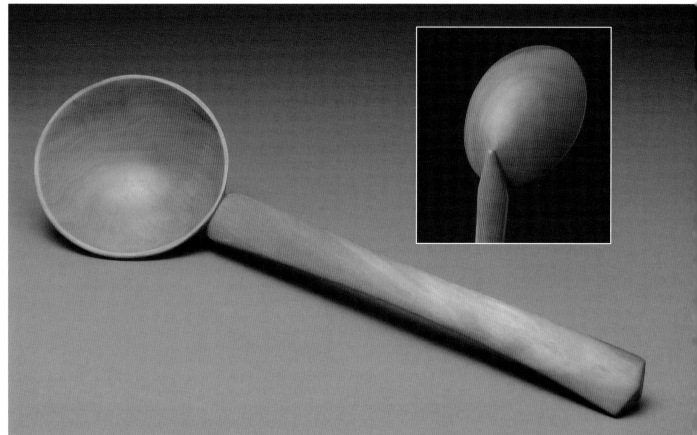

TOP:
Betty Scarpino
Indiana
2008
Persimmon

ABOVE:
Kent Scheer
Minnesota
2006
Apple

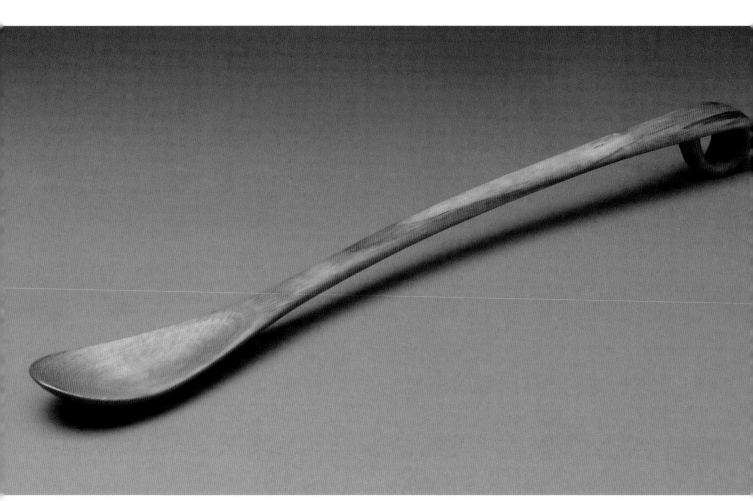

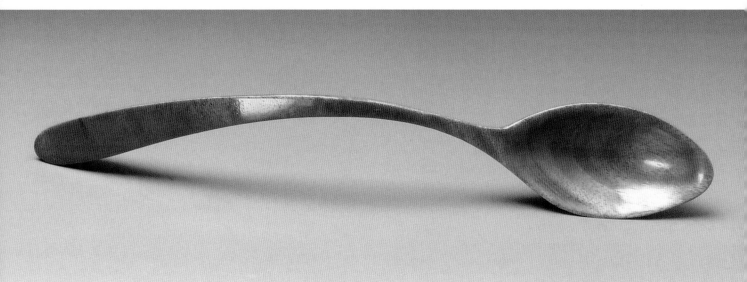

TOP:

Steve Schmeck
Michigan
2006
Buckthorn

ABOVE:

Michael Schwing
Maryland
2009
Mahogany

TOP:

Patty Scott
Virginia
2007
Basswood

ABOVE:

Nicolae Serban
Romania
Unidentified
2008

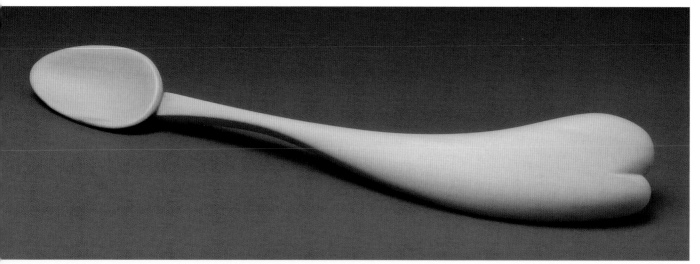

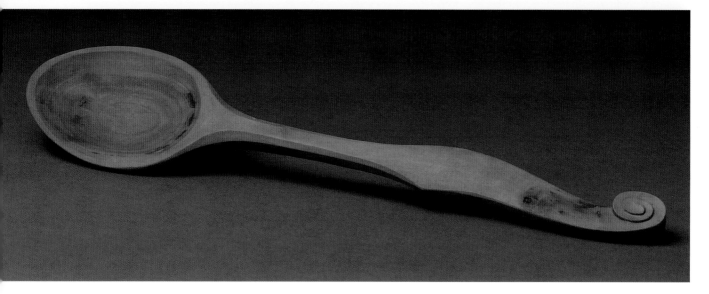

TOP:

Nik Sergeev
Australia
2010
Red gum

MIDDLE:

Mark Sfirri
Pennsylvania
2007
Alaskan yellow cedar

ABOVE:

Valdemar Skov
Maine
2008
Apple

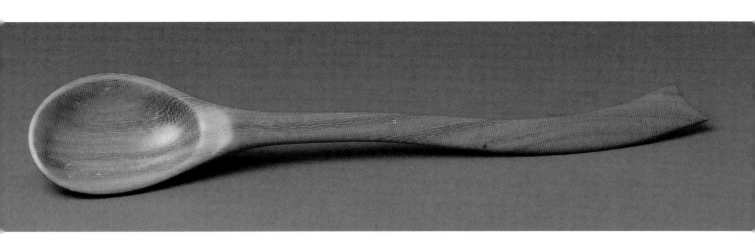

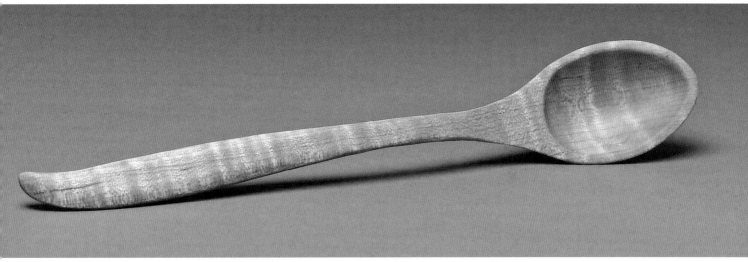

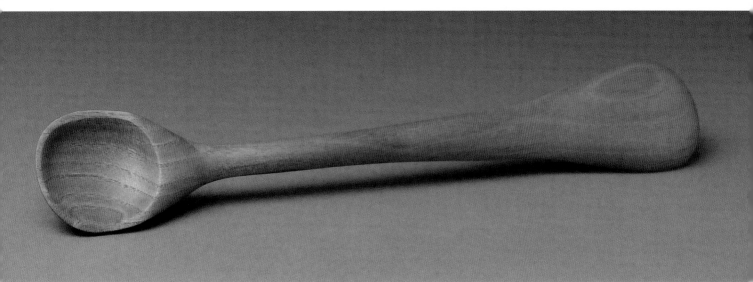

TOP:

Michael Smith
Pennsylvania
2006
Osage orange

MIDDLE:

Ken Snook
Pennsylvania
2007
Tiger maple

ABOVE:

Berte Somme
England
2007
Mulberry

TOP:

John Spinney
Maine
2009
Cherry

ABOVE:

Lebin St John
California
2007
Yew

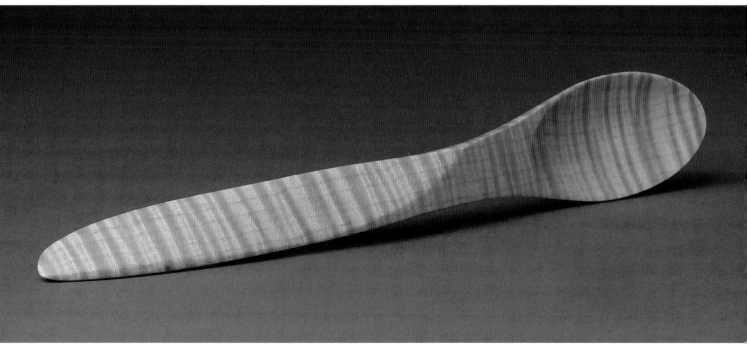

TOP:
David Stanley
Australia
2011
Saffron heart

ABOVE:
Mark Stanton
Pennsylvania
2010
Tiger maple

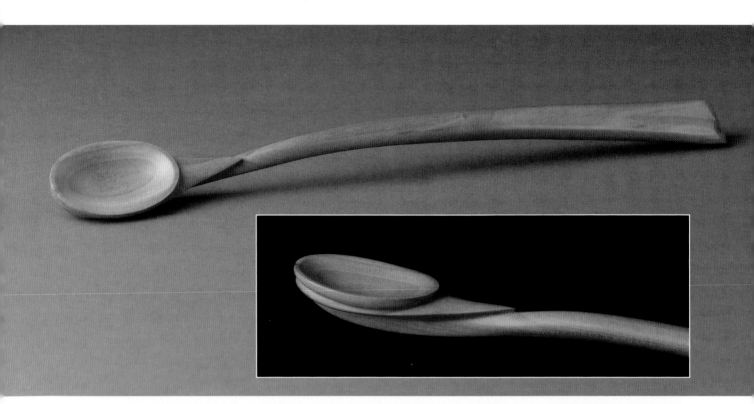

TOP:

Matthew Steel
New York
2010
Apple

ABOVE:

Del Stubbs
Minnesota
2008
Almond

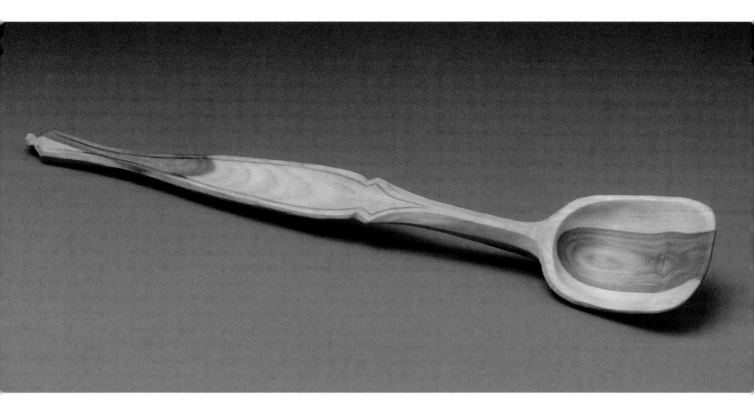

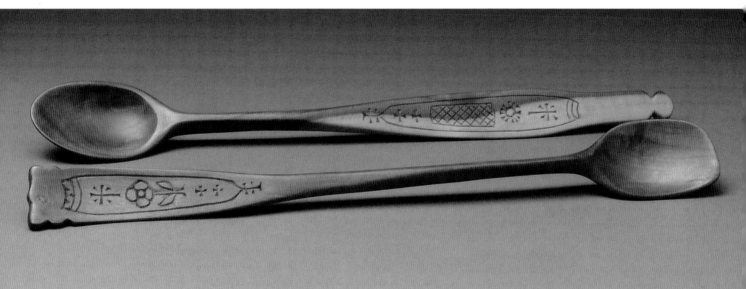

TOP:
Jögge Sundqvist
Sweden
2007
Lilac

ABOVE:
Wille Sundqvist
Sweden
2009
Lilac

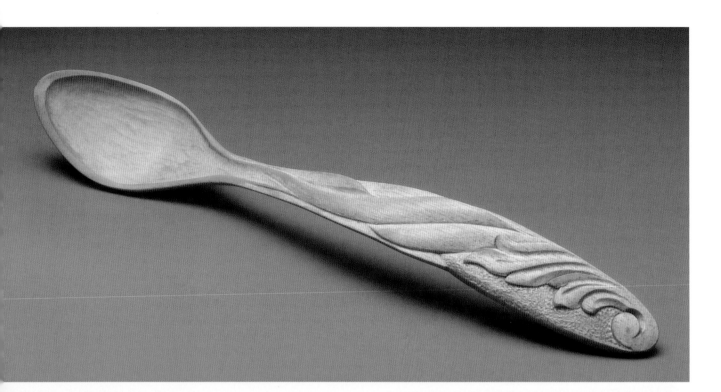

TOP:

Erno Szentgyorgy
New York
2007
Jelutong

ABOVE:

Masonari Takeuchi
Japan
2008
Chestnut

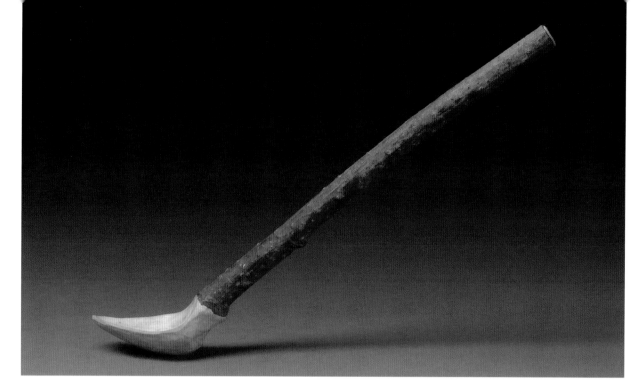

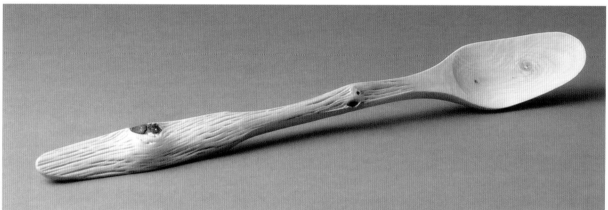

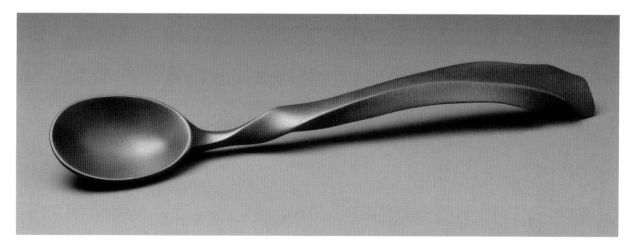

TOP:
Steve Tomlin
England
2011
Alder

MIDDLE:
Ian Tompsett
Czech Republic
2010
Hazel

ABOVE:
Holly Tornheim
California
2006
Manzanita

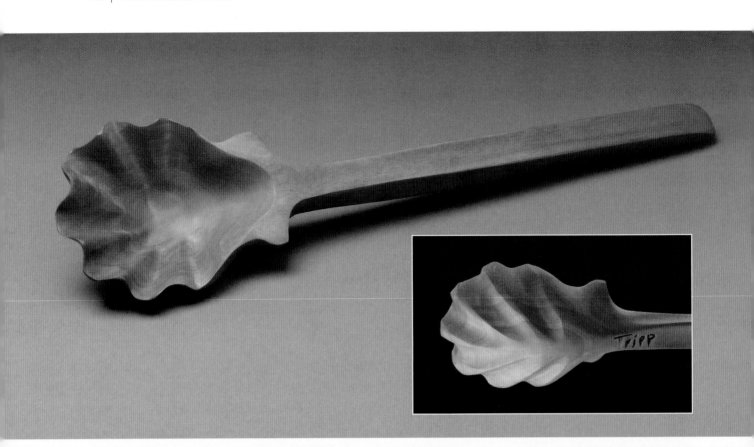

TOP:

Judy Tripp
Maine
2005
Cherry

ABOVE:

Joshua Trought
New Hampshire
2007
Spalted maple

TOP:

Gerrit Van Ness
Washington
2009
Boxwood

ABOVE:

Randy Van Oss
Florida
2006
Walnut

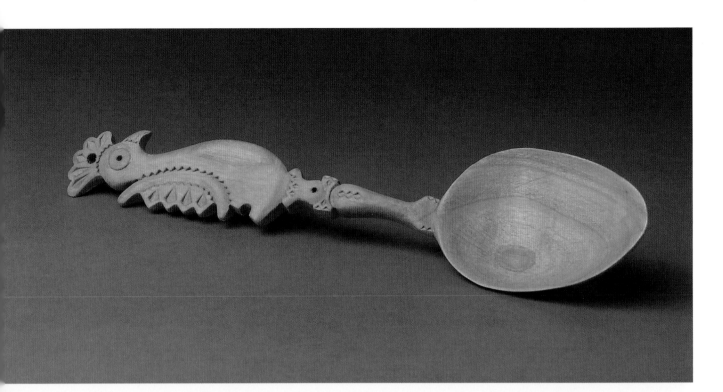

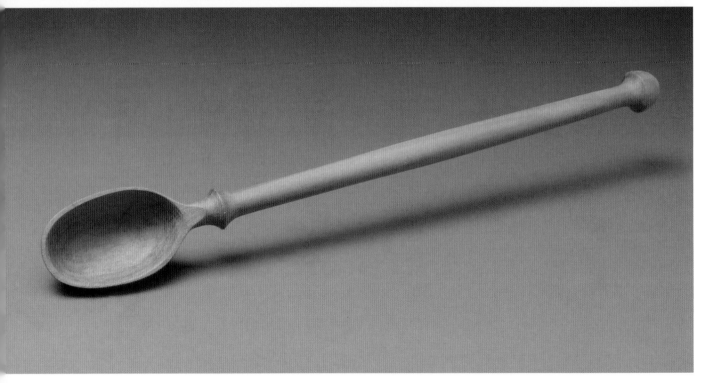

TOP:
Ene Vasile
Romania
2008
Beech

ABOVE:
Dick Veitch
New Zealand
2006
Kauri

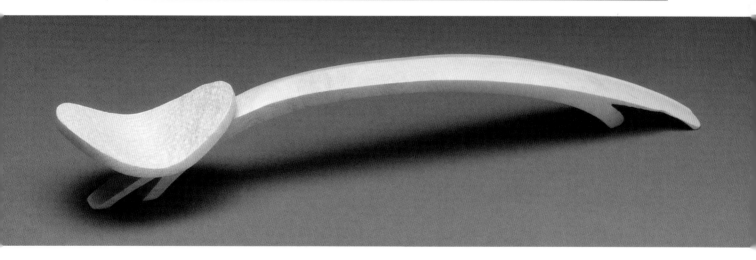

TOP:

Jacques Vesery
Maine
2010
Honey locust

MIDDLE:

Martin Viorel
Romania
2008
Cherry

ABOVE:

Amanda Wall-Graf
Oregon
2009
Holly

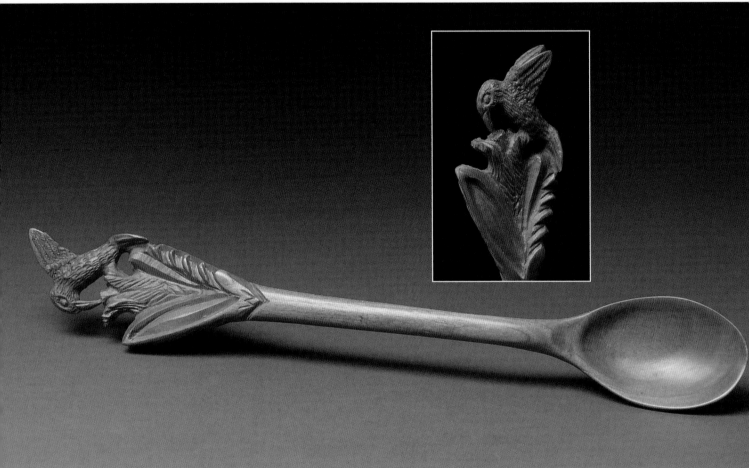

TOP:

Jason Weaver
Massachusetts
2009
Unidentified

ABOVE:

Rick Weaver
West Virginia
2008
Yellow poplar

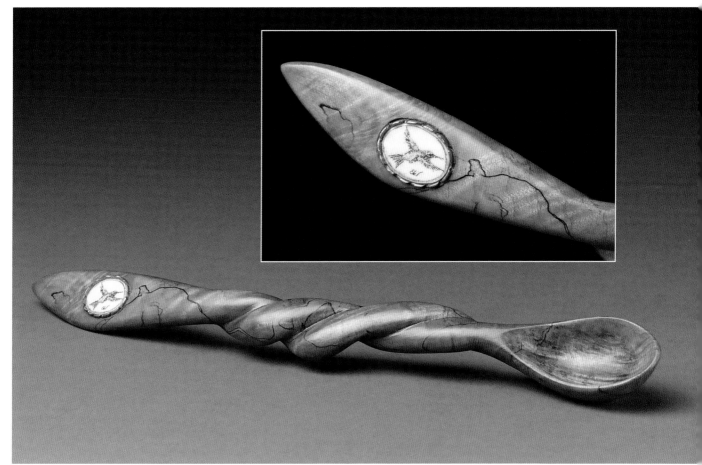

TOP:
Wes Weldon
Pennsylvania
2010
Black walnut

ABOVE:
Ed Wentzler
Pennsylvania
2010
Figured maple

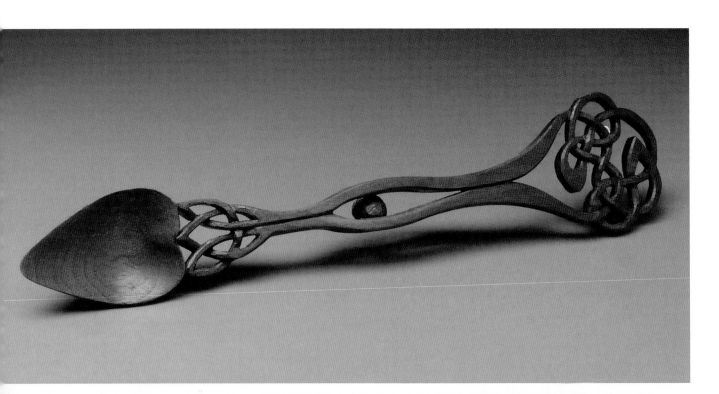

TOP:
David Western
Canada
2006
Black walnut

ABOVE:
Jay Whyte
Tennessee
2007
Cocobolo

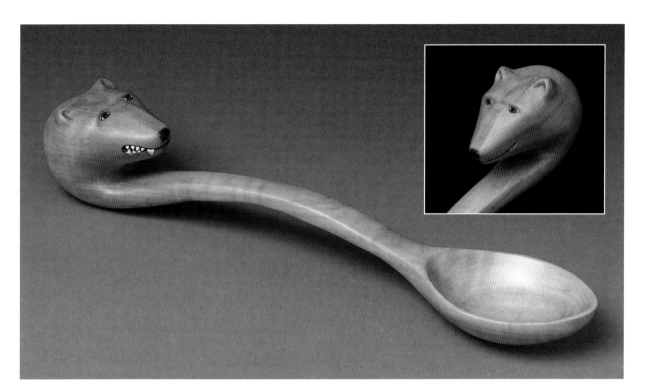

TOP:

Terry Widner
Florida
2009
Horse chestnut

ABOVE:

Charles Willard
New York
2011
Claro walnut

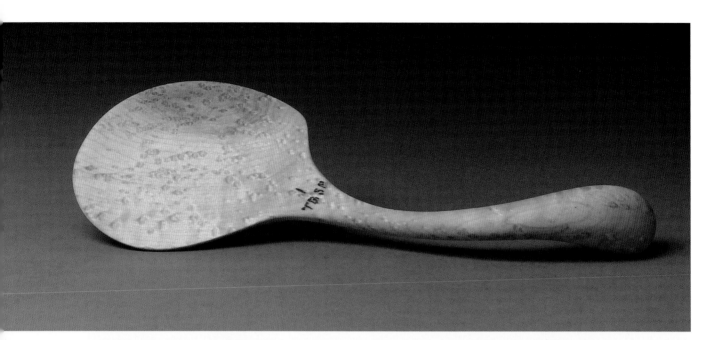

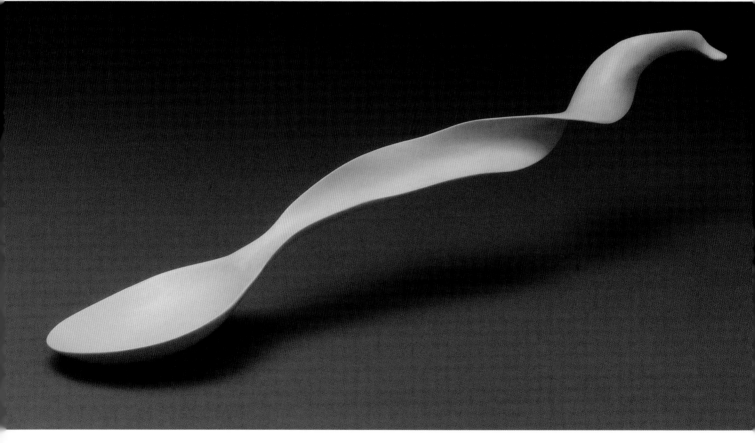

TOP:

James Wilson
Washington
2011
Curly maple

ABOVE:

George Worthington
New York
2009
Holly

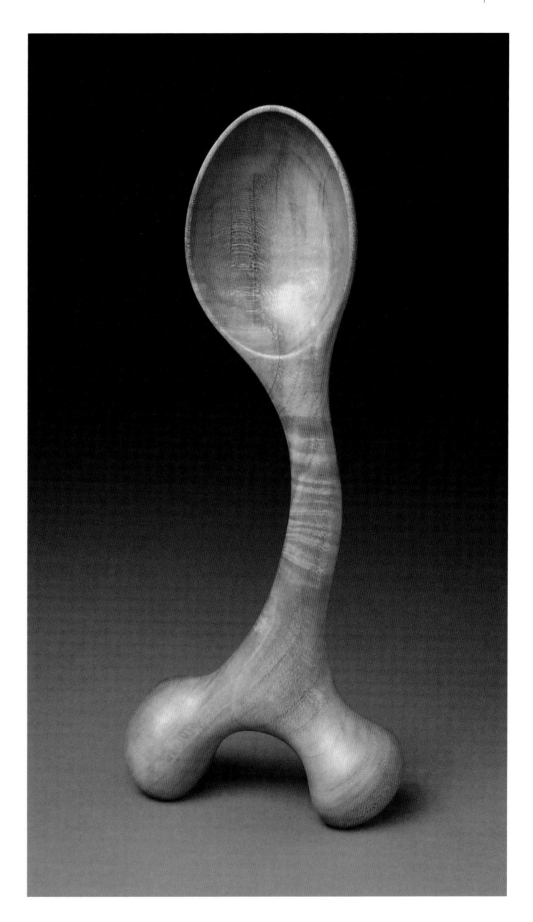

Frank Wright
Minnesota
2010
Maple

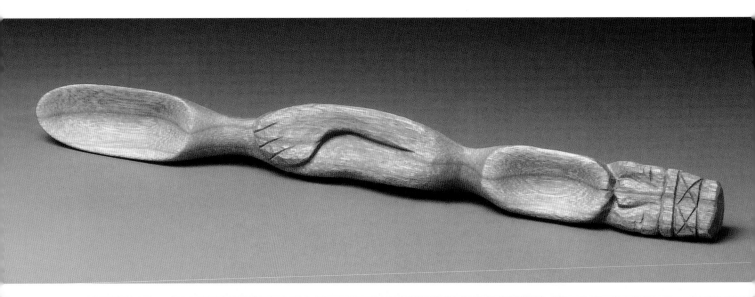

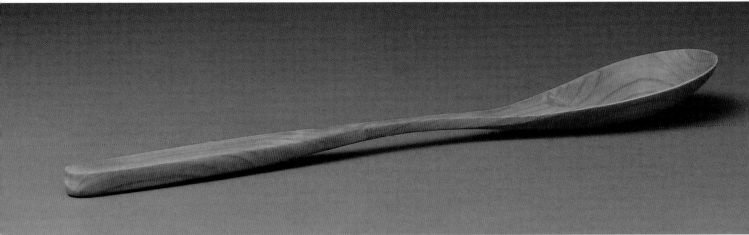

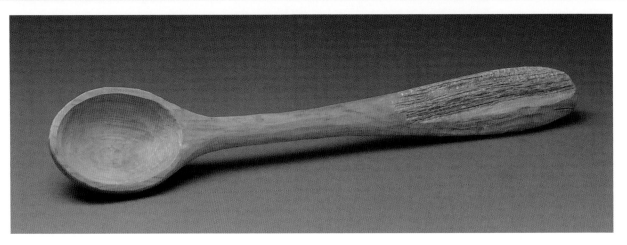

TOP:

Aki Yamamoto
Canada
2006
Cherry

MIDDLE:

Alan Young
Massachusetts
2008
Lilac

ABOVE:

William Zelt
Colorado
2006
Bristlecone pine

Selected Resources

There is such an enormous array of electronic, printed, and visual resources of potential interest to the various readers of this book that it is not feasible to attempt to provide a comprehensive listing. The resources listed below are ones likely to be of general interest to spoon makers at all levels as well as to spoon and wood collectors. My website, agatheringofspoons.wordpress.com, will provide, in addition to updates on the 9-inch spoon project and other information, ongoing information about these kinds of resources.

Inspirational and Philosophical Books

Murray Bail, *Eucalyptus*, Farrar, Strauss, and Giroux. 1998 (fiction)

William Coperthwaite, *A Handmade Life*, Chelsea Green, 2002

Roger Deakin, *Notes from the Walnut Tree Farm*, Penguin Books, 2009

Roger Deakin, *Wildwood: A Journey Through Trees*, Free Press, 2009

John Fowles, *The Tree*, Ecco, 2010

Jean Giono, *The Man Who Planted Trees*, Chelsea Green, 1985 (fiction)

Igor I. Gol'din, *Khorosha lozhka!* [The Handsome Spoon], Prosveshchanie, 1994

Harvey Green, *Wood: Craft, Culture, History*, Viking, 2006

Richard Horan, *Seeds*, Harper, 2011

Spoons and Spoon Makers

Paul Derrez, *Lepels/Spoons*, Galerie Ra, 2002

Ernest Hebert, *Spoonwood*, Dartmouth College Press, 2005 (fiction)

Hoezo Lepel?/What Do You Mean Spoons?, Museum Boijmans Van Beuningen, 2005

Tony Lydgate, *The Art of Elegant Wood Kitchenware*, Sterling, 1995

Dennis Ruane, *Wooden Spoons*, Hardwood Gallery Press, 2006 (fiction)

David Western, *History of Lovespoons*, Fox Chapel, 2012

Trees and Tree or Wood Identification

C. Frank Brockman, *Trees of North America*, Golden Press, 1968

Thomas J. Campanella, *Republic of Shade: New England and the American Elm*, Yale University Press, 2003

Herbert L. Edlin, *What Wood Is That?*, Viking Press, 1969

R. Bruce Hoadley, *Identifying Wood: Accurate Results with Simple Tools*, Taunton Press, 1990

Charles Fenyvesi, *Trees*, Avon, 1993

Romeyn Beck Hough, *The Woodbook*, Taschen, 2007

John D. and J. M. Lorette, *The Wood Collection*, Rare Materials Press, 2001

North House Folk School, *Celebrating Birch: the Lore, Art, and Craft of an Ancient Tree*, Fox Chapel, 2007

Russell F. Peterson, *The Pine Tree Book*, Brandywine Press, 1980

Terry Porter, *Wood: Identification and Use*, Guild of Master Craftsman Publications, 2006

Tony Russell, Catherine Cutler, and Martin Walters, *The New Encyclopedia of American Trees*, Hermes House, 2005

David Sibley, *The Sibley Guide to Trees*, Knopf, 2009

Henry Stewart, *Cedar: Tree of Life to the Northwest Coast Indians*, Douglas & McIntyre, 1984

Diana Wells, *Lives of the Trees: an Uncommon History*, Algonquin Books of Chapel Hill, 2001

Carving Techniques

Gwyndaf Breese, *Traditional Spooncarving in Wales*, Gwasg Carreg Gwalch, 2006

Dan Dustin, *Spoon Tales*, Dan Dustin, 2010

Herbert Edlin, *Woodland Crafts in Britain*, Batsford, 1949; David and Charles, 1973

Sharon Littley and Clive Griffin, *Celtic Carved Lovespoons*, Guild of Master Craftsman Publications, 2002

Rick Mastelli and Jögge Sundqvist, *Carving Swedish Woodenware*, Taunton Press, 1990

Dennis Shives, *Hand Carved Wooden Spoons*, Lulu, 2011

Judy Ritger, *Kolrosing with Judy Ritger Reviving a Lost Art*, Pinewood Forge, 2003

David Western, *The Fine Art of Carving Lovespoons*, Fox Chapel, 2008

Robin and Nicola Wood, *Wood Spoon Carving*, Stobart Davies, 2012

Electronic Resources

Many of the spoon makers featured in this book have their own websites, usually with useful information as well as color images of their work, so it is always worthwhile to search the Internet by name if you are looking for information about a specific individual's work.

eBay (www.ebay.com)

There are always a considerable number of spoons, often including work by contemporary spoon makers and relatively recent items listed on eBay. I have found the broad term "carved spoons" to turn up the largest number of results. eBay also has on its website, "A Short Guide to Spoon Collecting," that can be found in its Reviews & Guides Section (www.reviews.ebay.com).

Etsy (www.etsy.com)

Etsy offers access to a wide variety of contemporary hand made objects, including spoons, along with a ready means of contacting and exchanging images with participants. Commissioned items can be posted as reserved for a particular individual.

Pinewood Forge (www.pinewoodforge.com)

Del Stubbs is one of a number of makers of carving tools with websites through which to purchase those tools. His site is listed here because he also maintains a truly outstanding series of Spoon Pages that provide the most comprehensive one-stop resource with links to a fascinating array of wooden spoon information.

Country Workshops (www.countryworkshops.org)

Drew Langsner's North Carolina based Country Workshops is one of a number of websites that provide information about their wood workshops that may include specific courses in spoon carving. Country Workshops Woodworking School, for example, often has courses taught by the noted Swedish carver Jögge Sundqvist. Drew is also building an extensive collection of contemporary butter knives or spreaders, all of which are listed and described on his website.

Special Sources

There are a number of established craft teaching centers, like Country Workshops, in the United States as well as in England and other countries. The North House Folk School (www.northhouse.org) in Minnesota is one example. There are also ecological organizations, like the Center for Whole Communities (www.wholecommunities.org) in Vermont that occasionally offer spoon carving courses, often with well-known teachers like Bill Coperthwaite, who sometimes teaches at the Center for Whole

Communities. The Heritage Crafts Association (www.heritagecrafts.org.uk) is a good source of information about programs in Great Britain. Individual spoon makers, like Dan Dustin and Barry Gordon, may offer instruction on an individual or group basis. Prospective students may wish to contact a spoon maker in their area.

The Milan (Minnesota) Village Arts School (MVAS), in association with a group of outstanding Minnesota spoon makers, sponsors an annual two-day Spoon Gathering in early June. Nora and I attended one of the early Spoon Gatherings and found it to be, even for observers, a rewarding experience. Further information can be found on the MVAS website (www.milanvillageartsschool.org).

In August 2012, Barn Carder and Robin Wood held the first Spoonfest in England. An international celebration of the carved wooden spoon, it seems destined to become a major event. Further information about the 2012, and future, programs can be found at http://spoonfest.co.uk.

A Gathering of Spoons Catalog and *Contemporary Wooden Spoon Makers: An International Directory*

As an essential component of the documentation of the nine-inch spoon collection, I maintain, as I have indicated, a catalog that provides a brief description of each spoon in the collection along with information about the maker, and a directory of the name, address, telephone number, e-mail address, and website (or as much as I have available) of spoon makers I have been able to identify. Both are works in progress that undergo regular updates and changes. At the moment I have no plans to publish that information in either printed or electronic form. I typically do print out a copy of the most current version of both of those lists to accompany any exhibit or display of the collection. I can send anyone, at no cost, the most current electronic version of either or both of those files as an attachment to an e-mail. I can also provide a one-time copy of either of those files at the cost, to be determined at the time, of printing and mailing. Please send requests to: normanstevens@mac.com, or 143 Hanks Hill Road, Storrs, CT 06268 (860-429-7051).

Photo Credits

All photos copyright Norman D. Stevens except for the following that are copyright American Association of Woodturners.

Albert, Joseph	Manesa-Burloiu, Zina
Anderson, Jim	Mangalan, Harry
Barrett, Abram	Manns, Ben
Binder, Jude	Marshall, Philip
Bizzarri, Elia	Pascal
Burke, Paul	Petrochko, Peter
Carlisle, Richard	Pyne, Ainslie
Chappelow, William	Randles, Dale
Chilcote, Dennis	Ritger, Judy
Cologon, Ray	Robishaw, Sue
Cook, Ronald	Ruane, Dennis
Coperthwaite, William	Russell, Jamie
Corbin, Martin	Sabrina, Amy
Dahl, Jarrod	Sannerud, Jim
Delp, Jon	Sartorius, Norm
Dangler, Tom	Scarpino, Betty
Dustin, Dan	Scheer, Kent
English, Mark	Schmeck, Steve
Fanelli, Deb	Schwing, Mike
Finkel, Doug	Sfirri, Mark
Foltz, Frank	St. John, Lebin
Free, Ken	Stubbs, Del
Garrett, Dewey	Sundqvist, Jogge
Gordon, Barry	Sundqvist, Wille
Gorman, Rick	Szentgyorgyi, Emo
Hardt, Connie	Takeuchi, Masonari
Helgager, Ray	Tornheim, Holly
Hibbert, Louise	Tripp, Judy
Hill, Jim	Van Ness, Gerrit
Hopkins, Rodney	Van Oss, Randy
Jensen, Paul	Veitch, Dick
Judkins, Vern	Vesery, Jacques
Klein, Rich	Wall-Graf, Amanda
Latane, Tom	Western, David
Lively, Deborah	Whyte, Jay
Livesay, Fred	Widner, Terry
Loewen, Barry	Worthington, George

Tib Shaw is the curator of the American Association of Woodturners Gallery of Wood Art in Saint Paul, Minnesota, as well as a freelance photographer. She holds a bachelor of fine arts degree in Media Arts.

Norman D. Stevens is Director of University Libraries, Emeritus at the University of Connecticut in Storrs, Connecticut. He, and his wife Nora, have collected a variety of contemporary crafts since they moved to Connecticut more than forty years ago.